Longman Biology homework for Edexcel IGCSE

Ann Fullick

Pearson Education
Edinburgh Gate
Harlow
Essex
CM20 2JE

and Associated Companies throughout the world

www.longman.co.uk

© Pearson Education Limited 2007

The rights of Ann Fullick to be identified as the author of this work have been asserted by her in accordance with the Copyright, Designs and Patents Act, 1988.

All rights reserved. No part of this publication may be reproduced, stored in a retrieval system, or transmitted in any form or by any means, electronic, mechanical, photocopying, recording, or otherwise without prior written permission of the Publishers or a licence permitting restricted copying in the United Kingdom issued by the Copyright Licensing Agency Ltd, Saffron House, 6–10 Kirby Street, London, EC1N 8TS.

ISBN: 978 1 4058 7493 9

Development and editorial by Sue Kearsey
Designed by Redmoor Design, Tavistock, Devon
Cover photo ©www.istockphoto.com/Sebastian Kaulitzki
Printed in Great Britain by Henry Ling Ltd., at the Dorset Press, Dorchester, Dorset

Acknowledgements
Q1 p.44: The graph of Global loss of sea food species was published in Worm et al. *Impacts of biodiversity loss on ocean ecosystem services*, Science vol. 314, no. 5800, 3 Nov. 2006, pp.787–790.
Q3 p.54: The table of crops lost to disease and pests 1988–1990 was published in Oerke et al. 1999 *Crop production and crop protection*, pp 691–741, copyright Elsevier, 1999.

Every effort has been made to trace and acknowledge ownership of copyright. If any have been overlooked, the publisher will be pleased to make the necessary changes at the earliest opportunity.

Contents

			How to use this book	5
Chapter 1		1	This is your life	7
		2	Maintaining life	8
		3	Speeding things up	9
		4	Releasing energy	10
Chapter 2		5	The variety of life	11
Chapter 3		6	The breath of life	12
		7	Exchanging gases	13
Chapter 4		8	Healthy eating	14
		9	Cutting food down to size	15
		10	Getting food into the body	16
Chapter 5		11	Blood – supplying your body's needs	17
		12	On the beat	18
		13	Fit for life	19
Chapter 6		14	Responding to change	20
		15	The way of seeing	21
Chapter 7		16	Staying in control	22
Chapter 8		17	Cleaning the bloodstream	23
		18	Keeping warm and staying cool	24
Chapter 9		19	Human reproduction	25
		20	The menstrual cycle	26
Chapter 10		21	The energy factory	27
		22	Plant design	28
		23	Bigger and better crops	29
		24	How does your garden grow?	30
Chapter 11		25	Watering holes	31
		26	Absorbing roots	32
Chapter 12		27	Plant growth responses	33
Chapter 13		28	Plant reproduction	34
		29	Fertilisation and dispersal	35
Chapter 14		30	Community life	36
		31	What is eating what?	37
		32	Biomass and energy	38
		33	Removing nature's waste	39
		34	Chemical merry-go-round	40
		35	Nutrient cycles	41
		36	Life in the balance	42
Chapter 15		37	Farming and pest control	43
		38	Food production and forestry	44
		39	A global threat	45
		40	Polluting the air	46
		41	Water pollution	47
Chapter 16		42	Similarities and differences	48
		43	Mutation	49

Contents

Chapter 17	44	Division and inheritance	50	
Chapter 18	45	Patterns of inheritance	51	
	46	Genetic problems	52	
Chapter 19	47	Natural selection in action	53	
Chapter 20	48	Selecting the best	54	
	49	High technology breeding	55	
Chapter 21	50	Using microorganisms	56	
Chapter 22	51	Genetic modification	57	
	52	Biotechnology	58	
		Glossary	59	

How to use this book

How to use this book

This homework book is designed to help you practise all the science you need for your GCSE. The questions are arranged to match the chapters in your Student's Book, as shown in the contents list for this book.

The questions will help you to:
- develop your ideas about each topic
- make key notes or diagrams to use when you revise
- practise solving science problems
- get information from tables, charts and graphs
- see how science affects you and your environment.

The questions are graded on each page, starting with simple exercises and getting harder. Higher tier material is clearly marked with square question numbers. Your teacher will tell you which questions to try.

Most of the information you need will be on the page with the questions, including formulae for calculations. Anything else you need will be at the back of the book. The questions are to help you learn, not to try to catch you out.

Remember Don't be content with just writing down an answer. Think carefully – does your answer make sense? Could you explain it to somebody else? As you do each question, you should: read, think, do, check – and finally understand! If you are still in doubt, ask your friends or your teacher, but work through the answer to make sure you really understand how to get there yourself.

1 This is your life

① Copy and complete these sentences. Use the words below to fill in the gaps.
excrete   move   reproduce   respiration   sensitivity   seven

There are .... life processes common to all living organisms. They all need food, and release energy from food by .... All living organisms .... to get rid of waste and .... all or part of their body. When organisms .... they make more of themselves, and these offspring grow to adult size. Living organisms react to changes in their surroundings – they show ....

② Non-living things can be similar in some ways to living things. Copy and complete this table to show which of the seven life processes each thing carries out. The first one has been done for you.

Life process	salmon	concrete	car	pig
needs food	✔			
respires using oxygen	✔			
excretes	✔			
reproduces	✔			
grows	✔			
moves	✔			
is sensitive to surroundings	✔			

③ The diagram below shows two types of cell from the human body.

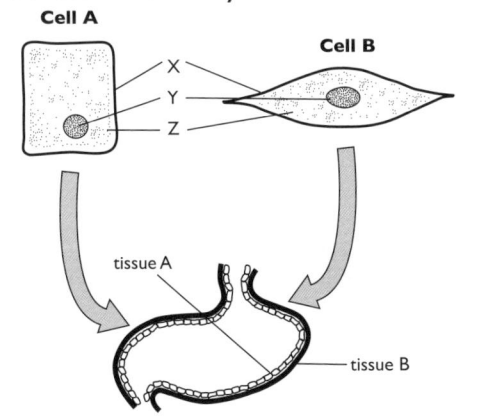

a Copy cell A and cell B and label parts X, Y and Z.
b What are the jobs of parts X, Y and Z?
c What type of cell is
   i cell A   **ii** cell B?
d Tissues made of cells of types A and B work together in an organ known as the stomach. What is the job in the stomach of
   i tissue A   **ii** tissue B?
e Which organ system is the stomach part of?

④ The diagram shows cells that are specialised to carry out a particular function (job) in the body.

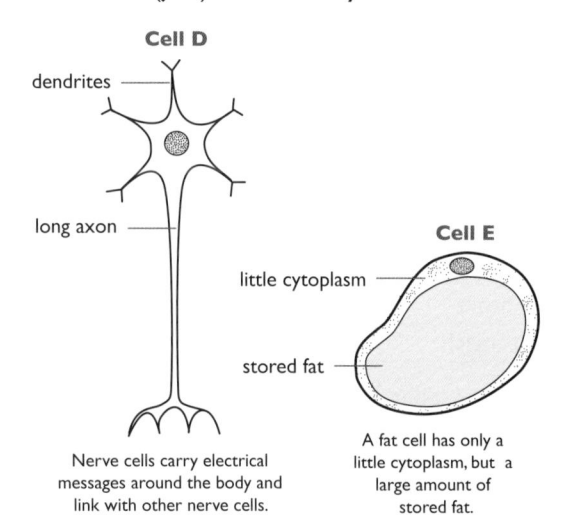

Cell D — dendrites, long axon
Nerve cells carry electrical messages around the body and link with other nerve cells.

Cell E — little cytoplasm, stored fat
A fat cell has only a little cytoplasm, but a large amount of stored fat.

Draw and label cells A and B. Beside each drawing make a list of the ways in which you think that the cell's structure makes it particularly well suited to the job it has to do.

7

2 Maintaining life

1 Copy and complete these sentences. Use the words below to fill in the gaps.

excrete   movement   reproduce   sensitivity   slow

All plants and animals do seven things: they ...., respire, grow, ..., react to their environment and use food for energy. Some of these are easier to observe than others, and .... is one of the clearest. It is usually fairly fast in animals, and although it is usually .... in plants it can still be observed. Most living organisms move towards things that they need and away from things that are harmful, showing .... by responding to change.

2 Copy and complete this table to show some of the organs in the human body and what they do.

Organ	What it does
heart	
stomach	
	co-ordinates all the messages from the sense organs and sends out messages to the body
eye	

3 Like many animals, plants have organs to carry out particular jobs.

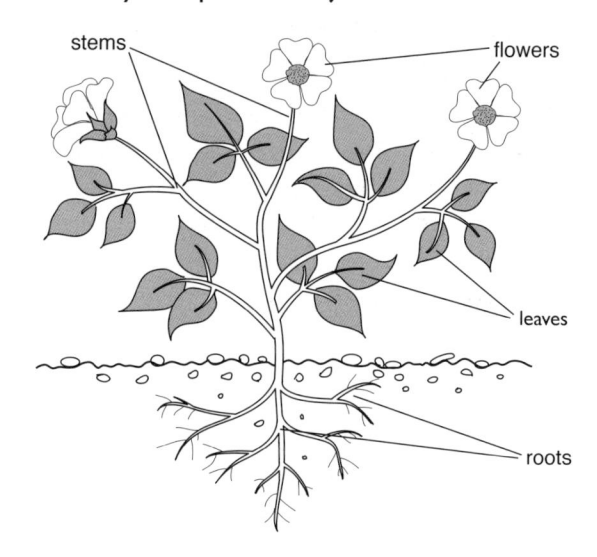

What are the main jobs of
a   the leaves
b   the stem
c   the roots
d   the flowers?

4 All living organisms need energy for the maintenance of life.
a   What do we call the process by which animals and plants release energy from their food?
b   Where do animals get their energy supply from?
c   How do green plants obtain the energy they need for life?
d   In a way all animals depend on plants for their survival. How do they depend on plants?

5 Our bodies need energy all the time to stay alive and work properly. Explain why we need energy
a   when we are asleep
b   for growing even when we are grown up.

3 Speeding things up

1 Copy and complete each sentence using the correct ending from below.
  a A catalyst will speed up or slow down a reaction …
  b Living organisms make very efficient catalysts …
  c All enzymes are …
  d The reactions that take place in your cells …
  e Digestive enzymes break down …
  f Each type of enzyme breaks down …

Choose endings from
  • wouldn't happen fast enough to keep you alive without enzymes.
  • made of protein.
  • large food molecules into smaller ones.
  • known as enzymes.
  • a specific type of molecule.
  • but is not changed itself.

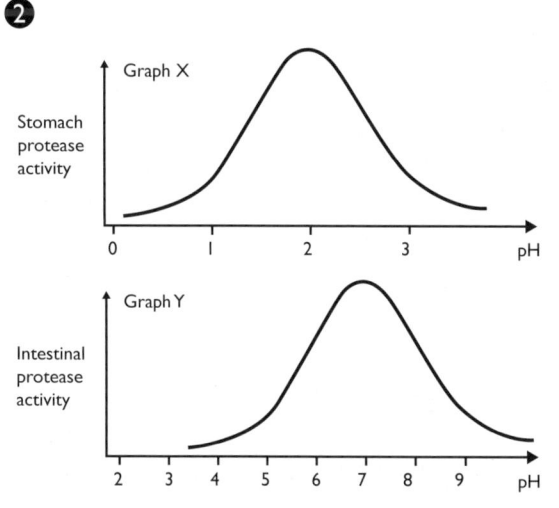

2

Graph X — Stomach protease activity (pH 0–3)

Graph Y — Intestinal protease activity (pH 2–9)

  a Graph X shows the effect of pH on the activity of the protein-digesting enzyme produced in the stomach. At which pH does this enzyme work best?
  b Graph Y shows the effect of pH on a protein-digesting enzyme from another part of the gut. At which pH does this enzyme work best?
  c The acid conditions of the stomach have an important effect on bacteria which may be taken in with the food. What is it?

3 Some students investigated the breakdown of starch using the enzyme amylase (found in the saliva in your mouth). In one test tube they kept starch solution at room temperature. In two other tubes they mixed the starch solution with the enzyme amylase.

They kept one of these tubes at room temperature and placed the other tube in a water bath at body temperature.

They took samples from each tube every minute and mixed them with iodine on a spotting tile. Iodine turns blue-black in the presence of starch. The results are shown in the diagram.

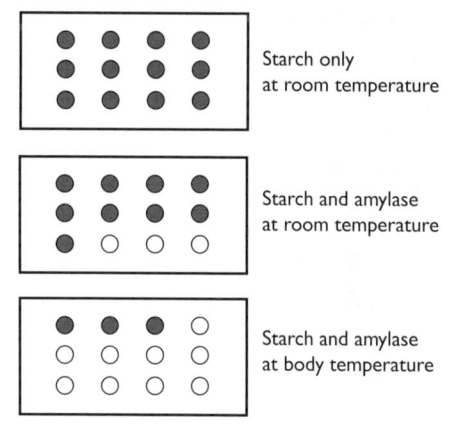

Starch only at room temperature

Starch and amylase at room temperature

Starch and amylase at body temperature

  a What effect does amylase have on starch? What is your evidence for this?
  b What do the results tell you about the effect of temperature on the action of the enzyme amylase?
  c Why is one tube of starch solution kept at room temperature without the addition of the enzyme?
  d What do you predict would happen to the activity of the enzyme if acid from the stomach was added to the mixture? Explain your answer.

4 Releasing energy

1 Copy and complete these sentences. Use the words below to fill in the gaps.
energy food fuels glucose heat

When .... like coal burn they release their stored energy as .... Living organisms use .... as their fuel. The main fuel which provides your body with the .... it needs is ....

2 Copy out and complete each sentence using the correct ending from below.
 a Energy is released from glucose …
 b During respiration chemical reactions take place …
 c When glucose reacts with oxygen, …
 d In respiration, carbon dioxide and water …
 e Because it uses oxygen from the air the process …

Choose endings from
• energy is released.
• is known as aerobic respiration.
• are formed as waste products.
• by a process called respiration.
• inside the cells of your body.

3 It is very important for your body to have a regular supply of food to provide energy for your cells. If you don't get enough to eat you become thin and stop growing. You will become weak and tired, not wanting to move around and you will start to feel very cold.

What are the three main uses of the energy released in your body during respiration?

4 a Copy and complete the sentences at the top right, choosing the correct word from each pair.

Oxygen/ozone and **glycogen/glucose** react together in your body to produce **excretion/energy**. This process is **respiration/breathing**. **Carbon dioxide/carbon monoxide** and **waste/water** are produced as by-products of respiration.
 b Copy and fill in the gaps in this equation for aerobic respiration. Use part **a** to help you.

.... + ... → .... + ... + ...

5 When you move around normally you produce the energy your body needs from aerobic respiration. If you are exercising hard, and there is not enough oxygen reaching your muscles, your body gets some of its energy from anaerobic respiration.
 a Write a word equation for anaerobic respiration.
 b What is the main advantage of anaerobic respiration?
 c What is the main disadvantage of anaerobic respiration?
 d Explain why you continue to breathe heavily for a while after hard exercise.

6 Two beakers are set up, each containing water and a crystal of purple potassium manganate(VII). The temperature of the water in beaker A is 10 °C. In beaker B the water temperature is 20 °C.
 a What would you expect to see happen in beaker A?
 b i Which physical process is responsible for the changes you see called?
  ii Explain how the process results in the spread of the purple colour.
 c What differences would you expect to see between beaker A and beaker B?
 d Explain these differences as fully as you can.

10

5 The variety of life

1 For many years people thought there were only two kingdoms in the living world – the plants and the animals. Although we now know there are other kingdoms, the plants and the animals are still grouped according to their main characteristics.

  a Copy and complete this table to show the main characteristics of the plants and the animals.

Characteristic	Plants	Animals
single/ multicellular?	i	multicellular
choroplasts?	ii	iii
cell wall present?	iv	v
food source	vi	vii
main carbohydrate storage compound	starch	viii
movement	ix	x

  b What is the main difference between a vertebrate and an invertebrate animal?

2 a Name two different types of fungi.
  b How do fungi differ from plants?
  c Explain the following terms.
    i hyphae
    ii mycelium
    iii spore

3 a Draw and label a yeast cell.
  b Draw and label one hypha of a mould such as *Mucor*.
  c A fungus such as *Mucor* has a special way of obtaining its food.
    i Describe how *Mucor* obtains its food.
    ii What is this method of feeding called?

4 Bacteria and viruses are very small. Bacteria have a structure a bit like a plant cell with a cell wall, but their genetic material is not in a nucleus. Viruses are smaller than bacteria and they are made up of a simple protein coat containing a small amount of genetic material.

Copy these diagrams of a bacterium and a virus. Use the information above to help you label your diagrams.

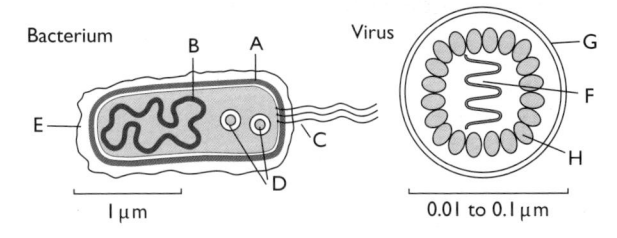

5 Bacteria and viruses are both microorganisms. However they are very different. Describe the differences between bacteria and viruses in
  a their size
  b the way they carry out the processes of living organisms
  c their impact on human life.

6 The breath of life

1 Copy and complete these sentences. Use the words below to fill in the gaps.
**alveoli   breathing system   lungs
carbon dioxide   diaphragm**

The job of your ………………… is to get fresh supplies of air containing oxygen into your …………………, and to get rid of waste ………………… produced by your body. Air is brought into the lungs by the movements of the ribs and the ………………… . Gas exchange takes place in tiny air sacs called ………………… .

2 Look at the words and definitions. Then copy out each word with its correct definition.

alveoli	the smallest air passages in the lungs
trachea	the upper part of the body containing the lungs
lungs	the main air passage leading in from the mouth and nose
diaphragm	the body organs where gas exchange takes place
bronchioles	millions of tiny air sacs making up the gas exchange tissue
thorax	large sheet of muscle separating the thorax from the abdomen

3 Gas exchange in the lungs works effectively when we move air in and out of the lungs regularly. We do this by breathing, or ventilation. Our breathing movements involve the muscles between the ribs and the diaphragm. Explain carefully, using words and/or diagrams, the events which take place
  a when you breathe in
  b when you breathe out.

4 The table shows the effect of exercise on the breathing rate of three people.

Activity	Number of breaths taken per minute		
	person A	person B	person C
rest	21	15	18
20 step-ups per minute	29	21	25
50 step-ups per minute	40	30	34

  a Plot a bar chart of these results to make it easier to compare them.
  b Which person do you think is the fittest, and which do you think is the least fit? Explain your answers.
  c What else happens to the breathing as well as the rate going up?
  d Why does our breathing change when we exercise?

5 The diagram shows the breathing rate of a young person taking part in a 400-metre race.

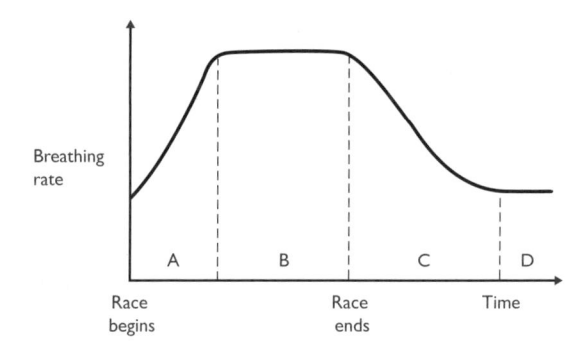

Use your knowledge of breathing and respiration to explain areas A–D on the graph.

7 Exchanging gases

1 Copy the diagram, and use the labels below to replace A–D correctly.

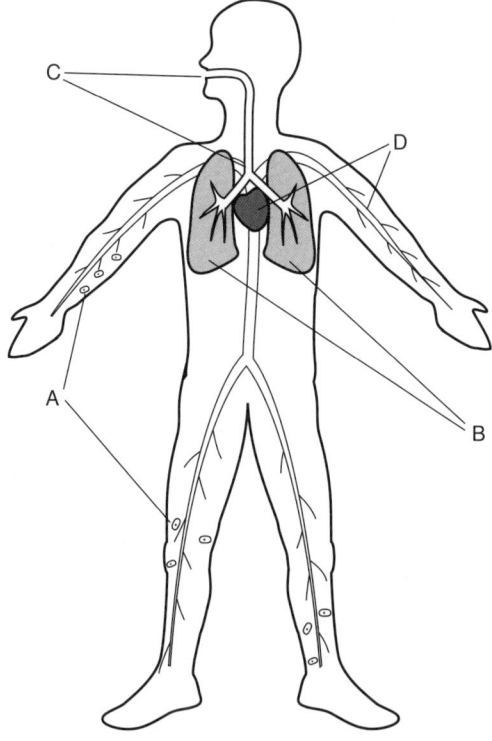

- You breathe to take air in and out of your body.
- In your lungs you exchange waste carbon dioxide from your blood and take in oxygen from the air.
- Your circulatory system makes sure blood brings oxygen to every cell that needs it.
- In your cells, respiration uses oxygen to release the energy from your food, making carbon dioxide and water as waste products.

2 The air you breathe in contains about 20% oxygen and only 0.04% carbon dioxide. The air you breathe out contains around 16% oxygen and 4% carbon dioxide. What happens in your lungs to bring about these changes?

3 Alveoli are very specialised structures to allow the exchange of gases in the lungs. The diagram top right shows one alveolus.

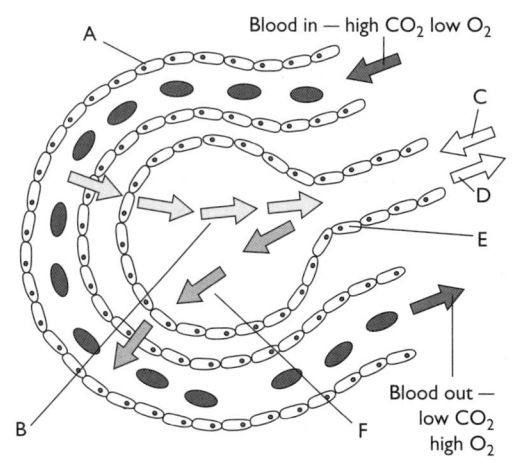

a Copy and label the diagram.
b Describe **three** features of alveoli which make gas exchange as effective as possible.

4 Smoking is bad for health.
a Name three components of tobacco smoke.
b Describe three ways in which tobacco smoke damages the lungs or other body systems.

5 Use the table to answer the questions below.

	Breaths per minute	Volume of each breath (cm³)	Pulse beats per minute	Volume of blood pumped out of heart per beat (cm³)
at rest	18	450	72	65
after 5 min gentle exercise	25	600	80	85
after 10 min hard exercise	41	1050	90	120

a Work out the volume of air (cm³) taken into the lungs over one minute
  i at rest
  ii after 5 minutes gentle exercise
  iii after 10 minutes hard exercise.
b Use your results from part **a** to draw a bar chart showing the effect of exercise on the lungs.
c Why is it so important that the amount of air taken into your body changes as you exercise?
d Explain briefly what happens to the blood flow through the heart during periods of exercise.

13

8 Healthy eating

1 Copy and complete these sentences. Use the words below to fill in the gaps.

**carbohydrates   chemicals   energy
fats   healthy   malnutrition**

It is important to eat the right amounts of food to remain fit and .... Food provides you with ...., and the different .... you need to keep your body working properly. The main food groups are ...., proteins and .... Eating too much, too little or the wrong sort of food can result in ....

2 Copy out and complete each sentence using the correct ending from below.
  a Carbohydrates are found in food such as …
  b Both carbohydrate and fats supply energy …
  c Fats are found in foods such as …
  d Too much, too little or the wrong sort of food …
  e Proteins, important for growth and replacing cells, …

Choose endings from
- cheese, butter and margarine.
- are found in meat, fish, eggs and pulses.
- cereals, fruits and root vegetables.
- but the energy in the carbohydrates can be used more easily by the body.
- causes malnutrition.

3 Kelly made a note of the food she ate one day.
- Breakfast: crispy rice cereal with skimmed milk and sugar, cup of tea
- Lunch: salad roll, cream bun, apple, water
- Evening meal: chicken, chips, sweetcorn, peas, apple pie, lemonade
- Snacks: chewing gum, bag of crisps, small orange

Copy the table and complete it using the foods Kelly ate. Note: some foods go in more than one place (e.g. the cream bun would go under protein for the bun and the cream, carbohydrates for the flour and sugar in the bun and fats for the cream).

Carbohydrates	Proteins	Fats

4 We get energy from all of the food we eat. But the balance of the different types of food we eat can affect our health – for example, it isn't healthy to get most of our energy from sweet things!

Government health departments issue recommended guidelines for different nutrient intakes. The table shows the recommendations for the proportion of energy adults should get from different food groups in three countries.

Country	Carbohydrate	Protein	Fat
UK	50%	15%	35%
USA	0%	10%	30%
Canada	45–65%	10–35%	20–35%

  a Suggest as many reasons as you can why the recommendations for the UK and the USA are different.
  b Suggest why the guidelines for Canada are given as ranges.
  c How useful are the Canadian values? Explain your answer.

9 Cutting food down to size

1 Copy and complete these sentences. Use the words below to fill in the gaps.

**bloodstream   digestive system
digested   enzymes   gut   mouth**

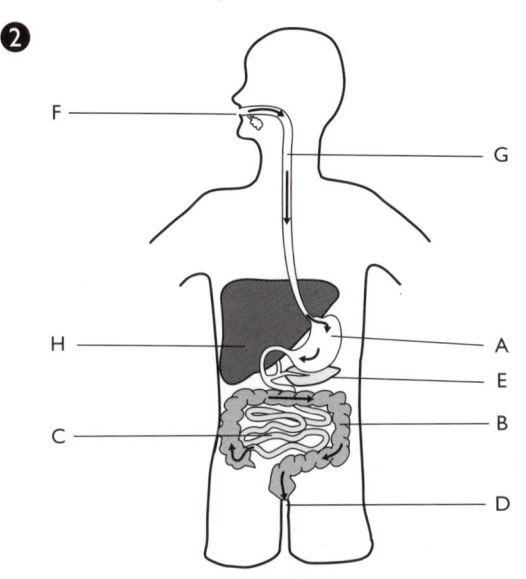

The food we eat cannot be used by the body until it has been broken down or .... This is the job of the .... Digestion begins in the .... and continues as food moves along the .... to other organs. Special substances called .... are produced in your gut to help break down the food you eat into small, soluble molecules that can be absorbed into your ....

2

(diagram of human gut with labels F, G, H, A, E, B, C, D)

a Copy the diagram of the human gut. Choose the correct label below to replace letters A–H.

**mouth   oesophagus (gullet)
stomach   liver   pancreas   anus
small intestine   large intestine**

b Write the function of that part of the gut next to each label.

3 Copy and complete the table to show the main digestive enzymes and what they do.

Name of the enzyme	What the enzyme works on	Products of digestion
protease	a	b
carbohydrase	c	glucose
d	fats	glycerol and e

4 Someone who eats a diet rich in fibre produce lots of faeces and food passes through their gut in about 24 hours. Someone eating a low-fibre diet passes much smaller amounts of faeces and food can stay in their gut for several days. Some evidence suggests the amount of fibre in the diet is linked with the risk of developing cancer of the bowel. However, other evidence suggests there is no link. Here are some of the data on which the scientific discussions have been based.

Number of men aged 36–64 suffering colorectal cancer per year (per 100 000)

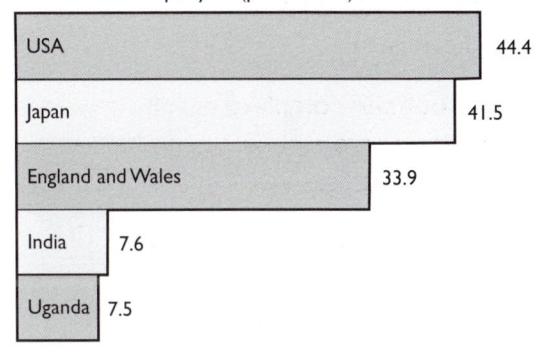

USA	44.4
Japan	41.5
England and Wales	33.9
India	7.6
Uganda	7.5

a In which two countries is bowel cancer most common?

b Draw a bar chart to show the data in the table below.

Country	% food high in fibre
England and Wales	64
India	87
Japan	85
Uganda	95
USA	64

c Which two countries eat most fibre-rich food? What is the incidence of bowel cancer in these countries?

d Which two countries eat the least fibre-rich food? What is the incidence of bowel cancer in these countries?

e Do your bar charts support the idea of a link between fibre in the diet and bowel cancer?

f What other evidence would you need to make a firm conclusion to your answer in **e**?

10 Getting food into the body

1 Copy and complete these sentences. Use the words below to fill in the gaps.
blood   digested   dissolve   gut   soluble

Once foods have been broken down to form small .... molecules, the process of digestion is complete. Molecules of .... food are small enough to be absorbed through the .... wall. They are also soluble so they will .... into the .... which transports them to all parts of the body.

2 a What is peristalsis?

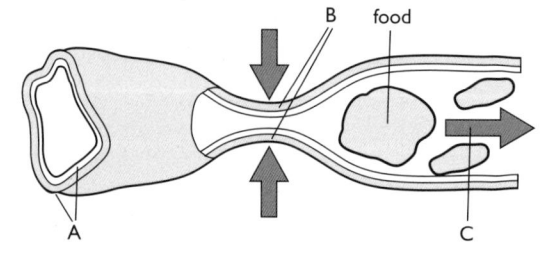

b Copy the diagram that shows food moving though the intestine. Replace labels A, B and C with the correct explanation below.
- direction the food is pushed in
- layers of muscle in the wall of the intestine
- muscles contract to squeeze food along

3 This diagram shows villi in the small intestine. Digested food is absorbed by the villi and passed into the blood to be transported around the body.

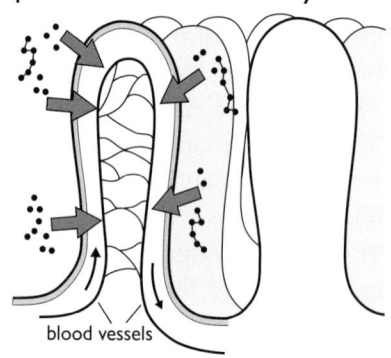

How does the structure of the villi enable food to be absorbed effectively in the small intestine?

4 You can make a model gut using Visking tubing. In an investigation students set up three model guts, each standing in a beaker of water.

In gut A they put starch solution. In gut B they put starch solution and the digestive enzyme amylase. Both of these tubes were kept at room temperature. In gut C they put starch and amylase and kept the tube at body temperature. They tested the water surrounding each model gut at intervals for the presence of both starch and glucose.

The students used iodine solution to test for starch. (Iodine solution is yellow when starch is not present and blue-black when starch is present.) They used Benedict's test to show glucose. (If the Benedict's solution remains blue this indicates there is no glucose present. If it turns orange/red this indicates the presence of glucose.)

The table shows their results.

	Iodine solution			Benedict's solution		
	after 2 min	after 5 min	after 20 min	after 2 min	after 5 min	after 20 min
Gut A	yellow	yellow	yellow	blue	blue	blue
Gut B	yellow	yellow	yellow	blue	blue	orange
Gut C	yellow	yellow	yellow	blue	orange	orange

Explain the results for each of the model guts.

11 Blood – supplying your body's needs

1 Copy and complete these sentences. Use the words below to fill in the gaps.

blood   circulatory   glucose   oxygen   heart   transported   waste products

Substances are .... round the body in the .... Food molecules such as .... and substances such as .... are carried to the cells where they are needed. The blood also collects and carries away .... from the cells. The .... system is made up of the blood, the blood vessels and the ....

2 Copy and complete the table, by replacing the bold letters with the words and descriptions below, to show the main parts of the blood.

Part of the blood	Description
a	The liquid part of the blood. Pale yellow and made mainly of water. It contains dissolved food molecules and other chemicals.
red blood cells	**b**
white blood cells	**c**
d	These are small fragments of cells with no nucleus. They help to clot the blood.

- platelets   • plasma
- These cells have a nucleus and help to defend the body against microorganisms that cause disease.
- These cells have no nucleus. They are packed with the red pigment haemoglobin which carries oxygen.

3 The red blood cells carry oxygen around the body. They can do this because they are packed with a red pigment called haemoglobin. This combines with oxygen to form oxyhaemoglobin. The red blood cells then carry the oxygen. In parts of the body that need oxygen, the oxyhaemoglobin rapidly breaks down to form haemoglobin and oxygen.

Copy and label the diagram to show where in the body oxygen is picked up by the red blood cells and where it is unloaded. Use the labels below on your diagram.

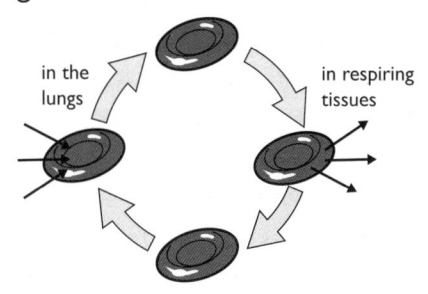

- oxygen in
- oxygen out
- red cells with oxyhaemoglobin
- red cells with haemoglobin (without oxygen)

4 The number of red blood cells in 1 mm^3 of normal human blood is around 5000 million. However, in some conditions the numbers of red blood cells in the blood may be much higher or lower than this. For each of the examples below, explain the difference in the red blood cell count and the effect it will have on the person.

a A person living at high altitude (where the air contains less oxygen) has a higher red blood cell count than someone living at low altitude.

b An athlete who has used the illegal practice of 'blood doping' will have a higher than normal red blood cell count. Blood doping involves taking blood from themselves, storing it for several weeks, and then putting it back into their blood system the day before a competition.

c A person who does not have sufficient iron in their diet will be anaemic. Their red blood cell count will be lower than normal.

12 On the beat

1 Copy and complete these sentences. Use the words below to fill in the gaps.
**circulatory system   pumps
blood vessels   capillaries   heart**

Blood flows around your body through a network of .... which are part of the .... Your blood is kept flowing by the action of the .... The heart is a muscular bag which .... the blood through the system. The blood vessels include the arteries, veins and ....

2 Copy and complete each sentence using the correct ending from below.
a Blood enters ...
b The atria contract and ...
c The ventricles contract and ...
d The blood leaving the right side of the heart ...
e The blood leaving the left side of the heart ...

Choose endings from
- force blood out of the heart.
- is pumped to the lungs.
- is pumped around the body.
- force blood into the ventricles.
- the heart through the atria.

3 The diagram shows the double circulation of the human heart. Use it to help you answer the questions.

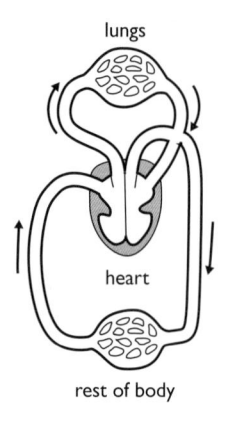

a Copy the diagram and shade it blue in the areas where there should be deoxygenated blood and red in the areas where there should be oxygenated blood.
b What happens to the blood in the lungs?
c What happens to the blood in other parts of the body?
d Why is it called a double circulation?

4 The diagram shows the main types of blood vessel.

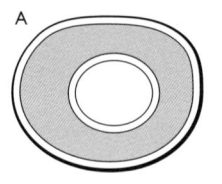

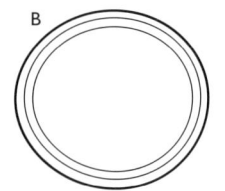

a Name each type of blood vessel.
b Describe the job of each type of blood vessel in the body.

5 Here are descriptions of two heart problems and how they may be overcome. Use what you know about the heart and the circulatory system to explain each problem caused by the condition and how the treatment helps.
a Sometimes a baby is born with a 'hole in the heart', which is a gap in the central dividing wall of the heart. The baby may look blue in colour and have very little energy. Surgeons can close up the hole.
b Blood vessels that supply blood to the heart muscle itself may become clogged with fatty material. This may cause chest pains when the person exercises, or they may even have a heart attack. Doctors may be able to replace the clogged up blood vessels with bits of healthy blood vessels taken from other parts of the patient's body.

Fit for life

1 Copy and complete these sentences. Use the words below to fill in the gaps.
**circulation   exercise   fit
healthy   heart**

Being .... is important – it helps to keep our bodies .... and lets us carry out all the everyday activities in our life. Regular .... improves your fitness. It has an effect on your muscles, ..., breathing and ....

2 These five sentences describe some of the effects of fitness on your body. Only three of them are scientifically correct. Choose and copy the correct sentences.
A Your risk of heart attacks and strokes decreases because of your improved circulation.
B Your breathing becomes shallower and you take in less air with each breath.
C Your muscles become larger and are able to work longer and harder.
D The risk of heart attacks and strokes increases because of the stress placed on your system.
E As your heart muscle becomes stronger your blood is pumped around your body more efficiently.

3 Regular exercise and getting fit is good for your heart and your lungs.
a Draw bar charts to show the data given in the table.

	Before getting fit	After getting fit
Amount of blood pumped out of the heart during each beat (cm^3)	64	80
Heart volume (cm^3)	120	140
Breathing rate (no. of breaths per minute)	14	12
Heart rate	72	63

b Use the information on your bar charts to explain exactly what effect increased fitness has on
  i your heart   ii your lungs.

4 Measuring the heart rate before, during and after exercise shows us what happens to the heart. The data in the table below comes from two 20-year-old students. Their resting heart rate was measured and recorded. They then exercised hard for four minutes, followed by a recovery period. Their heart rate was recorded every minute.

Time in minutes	Heart rate per minute	
	Student A	Student C
0 (resting)	75	65
1 (exercise)	95	85
2 (exercise)	115	105
3 (exercise)	135	125
4 (exercise)	160	150
6 (recovery)	135	120
9 (recovery)	105	80
15 (recovery)	90	65

a Plot a graph to show the heart rate of each student during the experiment.
b Explain carefully why these changes in the heart rate of the students occurred.
c How does the body control the heart rate and bring about changes like those seen in the graph you have drawn?

14 Responding to change

1 We have sense organs containing special receptors which allow us to detect changes in the world around us and inside our own bodies. Using this information we can react to our surroundings. Copy out and complete the table, using the descriptions given below to help you, to show some of our most important sense organs.

Poscition of the receptors	What the receptor cells are sensitive to
eyes	a
ears	b
c	changes in position, important for keeping our balance
tongue	d
e	chemicals, enable us to smell
skin	f

- light
- pressure and temperature changes
- ears
- sound
- nose
- chemicals, enable us to taste

2 Copy and complete these sentences. Use the words below to fill in the gaps.
**controls   stimulus   coordinates
senses   nervous system   receptors**

The human .... enables your body to detect and respond quickly to stimuli. A .... is a change in your surroundings or inside your body. Your .... make you aware of these changes using special .... which detect different kinds of stimuli. The rest of your nervous system .... all the information and .... the way your body responds.

3 The nervous system is made up of a number of parts. Explain the job of each of these parts.

a sense organs
b central nervous system
c sensory nerves
d motor nerves

4 a What is the main difference between a voluntary action and a reflex action?
b What is the value of reflex actions to the body?
c Analyse the following reflex actions using the sequence

stimulus → receptor → coordinator → effector → response

  i a doctor hits you just below the knee cap with a rubber hammer
  ii you put your bare foot down on a drawing pin
  iii someone claps their hands near your face.

5 The diagram shows the receptors, nerves and muscles involved in a reflex arc.

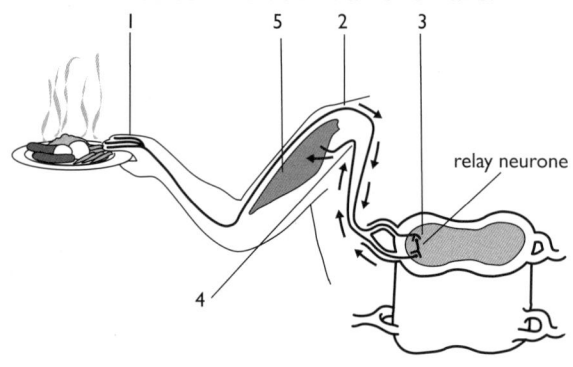

a Write a description of what is happening at each of the numbered points 1–5.
b How do you know consciously what has happened in a reflex action like this?

15 The way of seeing

1 The diagram shows the eye with some parts labelled.

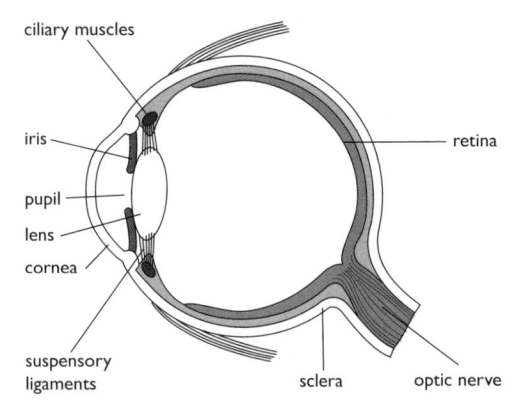

Copy and complete the table, matching the parts of the eye to the correct description of their functions.

Part of the eye	Function
a	contains receptor cells that are sensitive to light
b	tough white outer layer
c	muscle that changes the size of the pupil
d	curved transparent area that refracts light entering the eye
e	focuses the image on the retina
f	sensory neurones carry impulses from the retina to the brain
g	hole that allows light into the eye
h	change the shape of the lens
i	attach the ciliary muscles to the lens

2 The pupil of the eye is the hole through which light enters. The size of the pupil is controlled by the muscles of the iris and the pupil changes size depending on the light levels.
  a Draw diagrams to show what the pupil and iris of the eye would look like
    i in very bright light
    ii in ordinary light levels
    iii in very dim light.
  b Explain how the muscles of the iris change the size of the pupil.

3 Here is some information about three eye problems. Use what you know about the way the eye works to explain why these conditions affect sight.
  a With cataracts the cornea goes cloudy or milky.
  b Some people have an eyeball which is more egg-shaped than round. They are often short-sighted, and can clearly see objects close to them but not those at a distance.
  c If the retina of the eye becomes detached, people go completely blind in that eye.

4 Copy the diagrams and add to them to help you answer the following questions.
  a How do we focus on objects which are near to us?
  b How do we focus on distant objects?

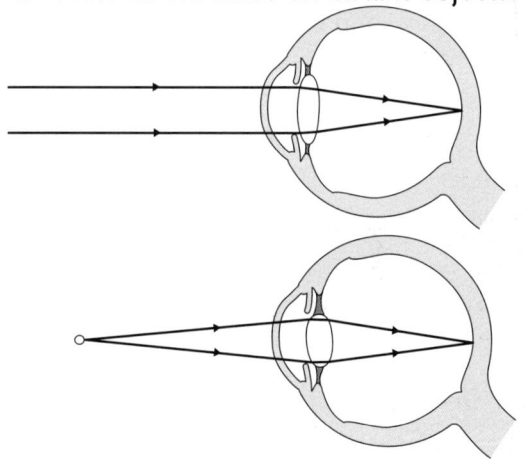

  c A scientist asked people to wear a special headset that seemed to turn everything upside-down. For several days they saw an upside-down world. Eventually they started seeing things the right way up again. When they stopped wearing the headset, everything appeared upside-down again. After a day or two their perception of the world returned to normal.

  Suggest what was happening at each stage of this experiment.

16 Staying in control

1 Copy and complete these sentences. Use the words below to fill the gaps.
**blood   chemical   electrical   glands
long-term   nervous   rapid**
Your .... system carries fast .... impulses. It is an important part of the .... response system of the body. Your hormones are .... messages secreted by special .... and carried around your body in the .... Hormones are often part of the .... control system of the body.

2 Match each word to its definition and then copy them out.

hormone   a condition when the pancreas cannot make enough insulin to control the blood sugar

insulin   a chemical message carried in the blood which causes a change in the body

diabetes   a hormone made in the pancreas which causes sugar to pass from the blood into cells where it is needed for energy

3 If you are excited, frightened or angry, your body releases adrenaline, the hormone which prepares you for 'fight or flight'. Adrenaline causes a number of changes to take place in the body.
  a List five of these changes.
  b For each of your answers in part **a**, explain how it enables your body to deal with a threatening situation.

4 Control of the blood sugar concentration in the body is monitored and controlled by insulin and glucagon from the pancreas. Draw and label a diagram that shows clearly how this control is maintained.

5 a Look at graph A. Explain why insulin in the blood increases after a meal.
  b Graph B shows someone who has developed diabetes but is not yet injecting insulin. What differences are there between this and graph A?
  c Graph C shows the effect of regular insulin injections on blood sugar of someone with diabetes. Why are the insulin injections so important to their health?

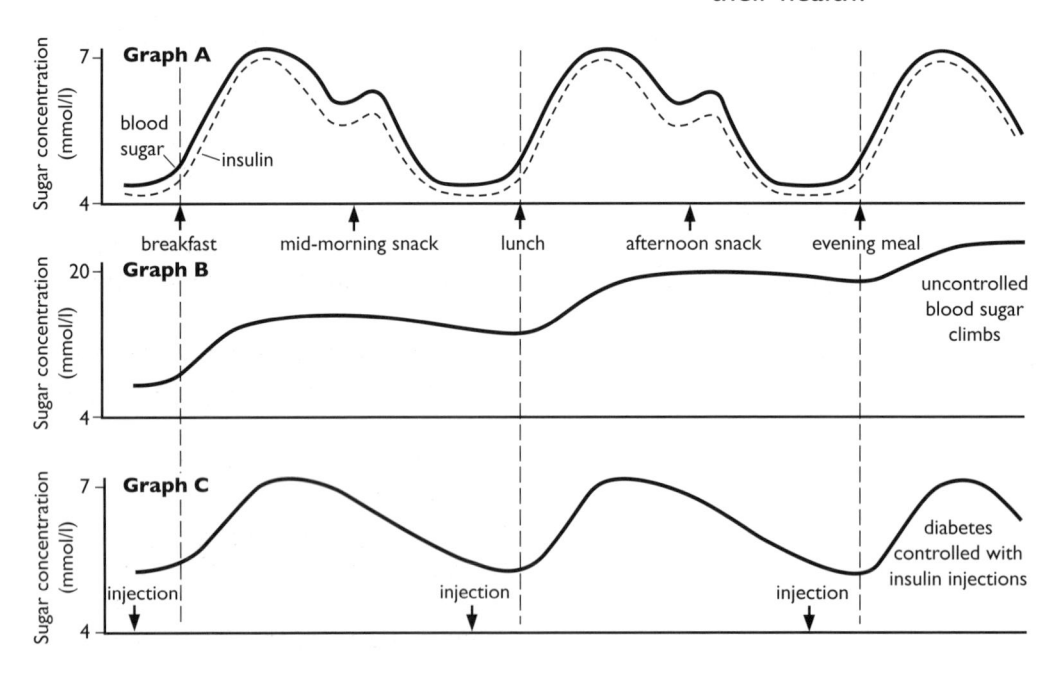

17 Cleaning the bloodstream

1 Copy and complete these sentences. Use the words below to fill in the gaps.
**amino acids   kidneys   lungs
respiration   urea   urine
waste products**

The chemical reactions which take place in your body to keep you alive produce .... which would be poisonous to your body if they were not removed. Carbon dioxide produced by .... is removed through the .... when you breathe out. Your liver breaks down excess .... (from proteins) to form .... This is removed from the blood by the .... and excreted in .... from the bladder.

2 If we take in a lot of liquid, the excess water is removed by our kidneys and we produce a lot of urine. Also, if we take in a heavy load of mineral ions, e.g. sodium, our kidneys get rid of the excess. But our kidneys are not the only way we control water and mineral loss.
  a Write down two ways that water is lost from our bodies other than in urine.
  b Write down the other way that excess minerals are lost from our bodies other than in urine.
  c How much glucose and protein would you normally expect to find in urine? Explain your answer.

3 Some of the substances in the blood flowing into a kidney tubule are glucose, dissolved minerals and urea.

Copy the diagram at the top right of the page and make a table to explain what happens to each of these substances at points A, B, C and D of the tubule.

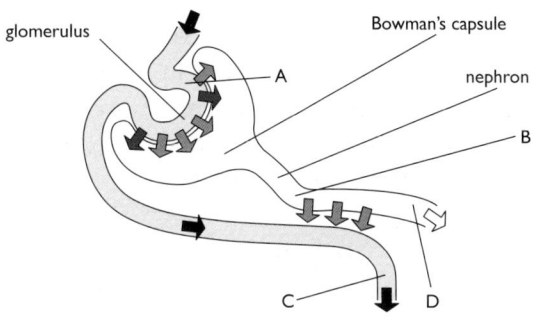

4 As part of an experiment a student drank some water. His urine output was then measured at 30-minute intervals for 150 minutes. The solute concentration of each urine sample was also measured. The graphs show the results.

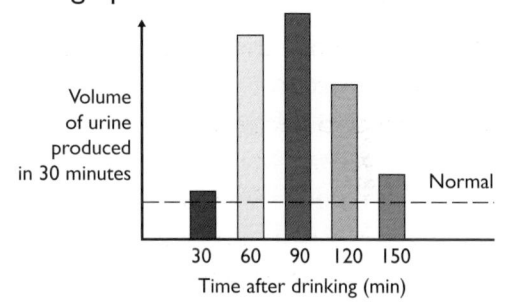

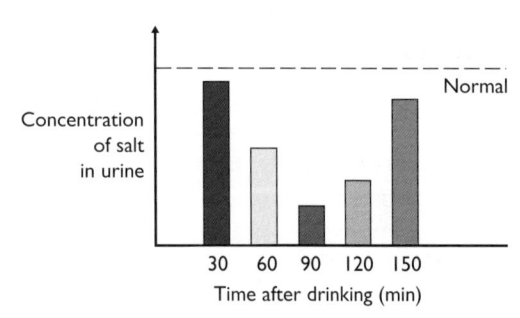

  a Describe how the volume of urine produced by the student changed during the experiment.
  b Explain how the hormone ADH is involved in the changes in volume of the urine produced.
  c Describe what happened to the solute concentration of the urine during the experiment.
  d Why do these changes in solute concentration happen?
  e What changes would you expect to see in the volume and solute concentration of the urine if the student did not drink for 12 hours?

23

18 Keeping warm and staying cool

1 Copy and complete the following sentences. Use the words below to fill in the gaps.

constant   die   enzymes   sweating

It is very important to maintain a .... internal body temperature of about 37 °C. This is the temperature at which most of the .... in your body work at their best. If your internal body temperature gets too high or too low you will .... You cool down by .... if your body temperature starts to go up.

2 a Rearrange these sentences to show how Sally's internal body temperature is controlled when it starts to increase. Copy the sentences out in the right order.
   A Her internal body temperature starts to rise.
   B Her temperature returns to normal.
   C Her skin goes red and sweating increases so the amount of heat lost through the skin goes up.
   D Sally exercises hard.
b What else would Sally need to do to return her body to normal?

3 Humans maintain an internal body temperature at about 37 °C over a wide range of environmental temperatures. Factors such as the thermoregulatory centres of the brain, sweating, vasodilation and vasoconstriction are all involved in this process. Animals such as fish, amphibians, reptiles and invertebrates cannot do this. Their body temperature is usually close to the environmental temperature.

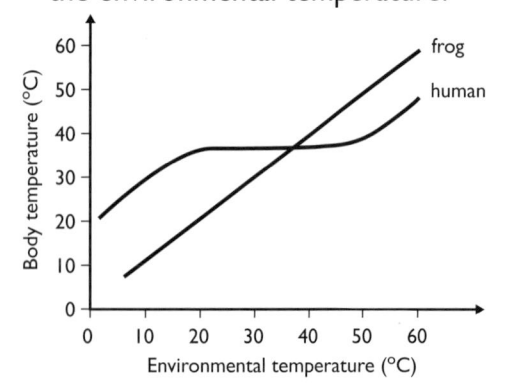

a From the graph, what is the body temperature of a human and a frog at an atmospheric temperature of 20 °C?
b At what external temperature does the human internal temperature become dangerously low? Why is it dangerous?
c At what external temperature does the human internal temperature become dangerously high? Why is it dangerous?
d Explain how a person maintains a constant internal body temperature as the external temperature falls.
e Explain how a person maintains a constant internal body temperature as the external temperature rises.

4 Hypothermia causes thousands of deaths in the UK every year. Use the information about hypothermia to design a poster to help people avoid this problem.
- Hypothermia is when the body temperature drops below 35 °C and the normal working of the body is affected.
- Old people, small children and people exposed in bad weather conditions are most at risk.
- Up to 20% of your body heat is lost through your head.
- Warm clothing, adequate heating, regular food and warm drinks and exercise all help to prevent hypothermia.
- People with hypothermia have greyish-blue, puffy faces and blue lips. Their skin feels very cold to the touch, and they will be drowsy with slurred speech. If the body temperature falls too low the sufferer will become unconscious and may die.

19 Human reproduction

1 Copy and complete each sentence using the correct ending from below.
  a The new individual formed in asexual reproduction …
  b In sexual reproduction special male and female sex cells fuse (join) …
  c The new individual formed in sexual reproduction …
  d The special sex cells involved in sexual reproduction …
  e A clone is the identical offspring formed …

  Choose endings from
  • are known as gametes.
  • contains a mixture of genetic information from both parents.
  • to form a unique new cell.
  • as a result of asexual reproduction.
  • is identical to the parent.

2 Puberty is the time when hormone-controlled changes take place in the bodies of boys and girls to produce sexual maturity.
  a What are the three main hormones which result in sexual maturity in boys?
  b What are the three main hormones which result in sexual maturity in girls?
  c Draw up a table to summarise the main changes which take place during puberty in boys and in girls.

3 a Copy the diagram of a front view of the female reproductive system. Use the labels below to replace A–E correctly.
  **cervix   Fallopian tube (oviduct)
  ovary   uterus (womb)   vagina**

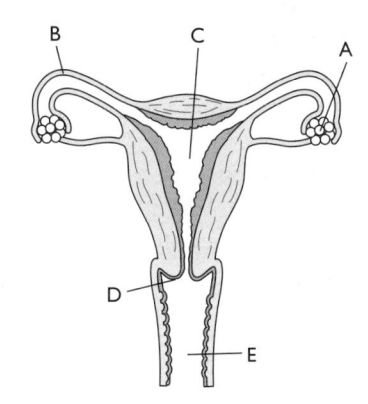

  b Copy the diagram of a side view of the male reproductive system. Use the labels below to replace A–E correctly.

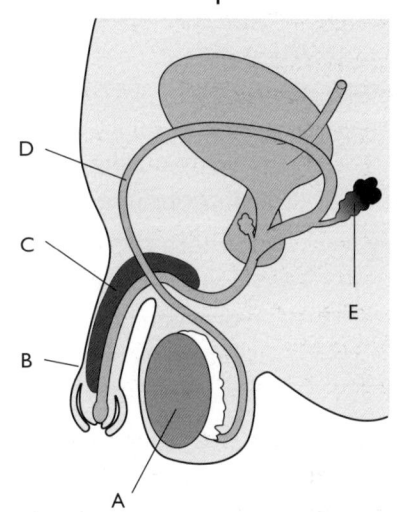

  **erectile tissue   penis   testis
  seminal vesicle   sperm duct**

  c Explain briefly but clearly
   i how an egg is fertilised by a sperm
   ii the role of the placenta during pregnancy
   iii the three stages of labour.

20 The menstrual cycle

❶ Copy and complete these sentences. Use the words below to fill in the gaps.
blood   hormone   ovaries   uterus

The monthly release of a fertile egg from a woman's ...., and the thickening of the lining of her .... in preparation for pregnancy, are controlled by hormones. A .... is a chemical messenger released in one part of the body and carried in the .... around the body to where it affects another part.

❷ Match each word with its definition and then copy them out.

pituitary gland	where sperm from a man's penis enter the body during sexual intercourse
ovary	where the fetus develops for 9 months; if no pregnancy occurs, the blood-rich lining is shed each month
uterus (womb)	small gland in the brain which produces hormones that control fertility by affecting the ovary
oviduct	releases a ripe egg each month and makes the hormones oestrogen and progesterone which control the menstrual cycle
vagina	the site where fertilisation of the egg by the sperm takes place

❸ Copy the diagram of part of the hormone system which controls the female menstrual cycle. Use the labels A–E on your diagram.

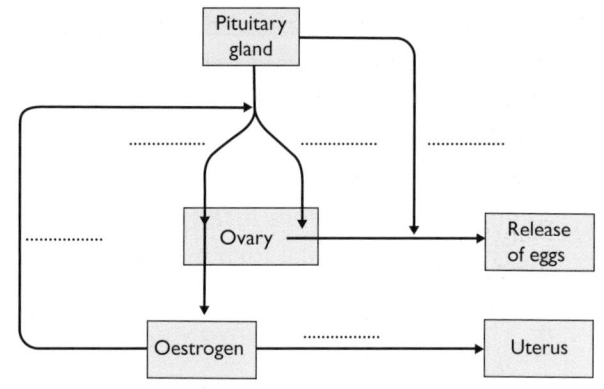

A FSH (follicle stimulating hormone) from the pituitary gland stimulates eggs to mature and ripen in the ovaries.
B FSH also causes the ovaries to make the hormone oestrogen.
C Oestrogen stimulates the womb to develop a blood-rich lining ready for pregnancy.
D Oestrogen stops the production of FSH. As the level of oestrogen rises, the level of FSH falls until the egg is released.
E LH from the pituitary gland stimulates egg release.

4 a Hormone treatment is often used to help overcome infertility. When FSH (follicle stimulating hormone) is used to stimulate ovulation, the dose must be carefully controlled. Why?

b If a woman has blocked oviducts, it may be necessary to harvest ripe eggs from her ovaries, fertilise them with sperm from her partner outside the body and then implant the tiny developing embryos back inside her uterus (in vitro fertilisation). Some of the embryos may be frozen and saved in case the pregnancy fails or in case the parents want another child later.

  i In this sort of treatment a very high dose of FSH will be given. Why?
  ii Oestrogen will be given as the time to harvest the eggs approaches. Why?

21 The energy factory

1 Copy and complete these sentences. Use the words below to fill in the gaps.
chlorophyll   chloroplasts   water photosynthesis   light   starch sugar (glucose)

Plants produce their own food in a process known as .... They absorb .... energy using a green chemical called .... which is found in .... in the plant cells. Carbon dioxide and .... are joined together using this energy to form .... and oxygen. The glucose produced in photosynthesis may be converted into insoluble .... for storage.

2 a Match each word related to photosynthesis with its description and copy them out.

carbon dioxide	is produced and released into the air
water	provides energy
sunlight	from the root moves up to the leaf through the stem
sugars	is absorbed from the air
oxygen	are made in the leaf and provide the plant with food

b Write a word equation for the process of photosynthesis.

3 Copy the diagram at the top right of a leaf. Use the labels A – E on your diagram.
A oxygen moves out
B the epidermis is a protective layer that lets sunlight through
C sugars dissolve and are taken to other parts of the plant
D stomata (pores) let gases in and out
E water brought from roots in xylem vessel

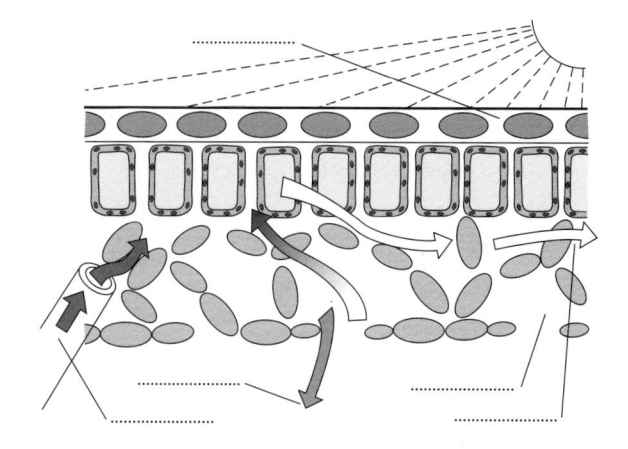

4 a Much of the glucose made in photosynthesis is turned into an insoluble storage compound. What is this compound?

b Some plants, like potatoes, develop special storage organs where they store food. One potato farmer recorded the overall amount of sunlight each month that her potato crop was growing. She also recorded the average crop of potatoes she got when she harvested the plants. The table shows her results. Explain what it shows.

Amount of sunlight	Mass of potato crop per plant
average	1.0 kg
poor	0.5 kg
high	1.5 kg

5 a Copy and complete the table to show three substances that may be made from the glucose produced during photosynthesis, along with what they do.

Substance made	Role/roles in the plant
i	storage compound
cellulose	ii
protein	iii

b The glucose made by photosynthesis is not only used to make other chemicals. What is the other main use of the glucose made in plants?

27

22 Plant design

❶ Match each plant organ with its description and copy them out.

leaves   anchor the plant firmly in the ground

stems   where sexual reproduction takes place

roots   use energy from light to make food

flowers   hold the plant upright and transport substances between other parts

❷ Copy the diagram of a typical green plant cell. Add the correct description to each label from the list below.

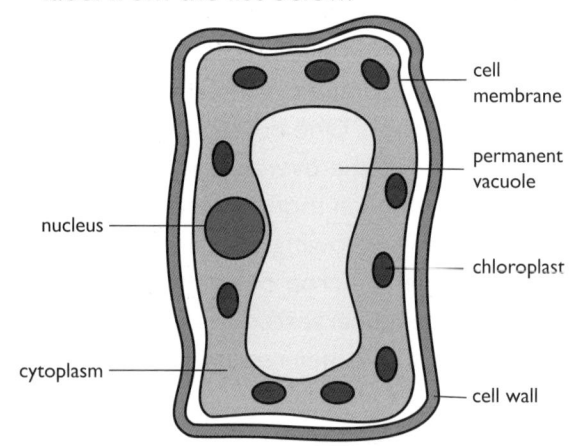

A controls all the activities of the cell
B where most of the chemical reactions take place
C controls the movement of substances in and out of the cell
D filled with cell sap and helps support the plant when full
E made of cellulose, it strengthens the cell and helps support the plant
F absorbs energy from light to make food

❸ Leaves are the plant organs that make food. They use light energy which is absorbed by chloroplasts.

Palisade cells contain lots of chloroplasts. They are packed tightly together in the palisade layer near the top of the leaf to absorb as much light as possible.

Epidermal cells cover the surface of the leaf. They are transparent so light can pass through them. They protect the leaf from water loss and damage. The lower epidermis has holes in it called stomata. Stomata can be opened and closed to let gases in and out of the leaf.

In the spongy tissue layer, the cells are packed loosely. They have a large surface area and there are big air spaces between them. This makes it easier for gases to move into and out of the cells.

Use this information to help you answer the questions.

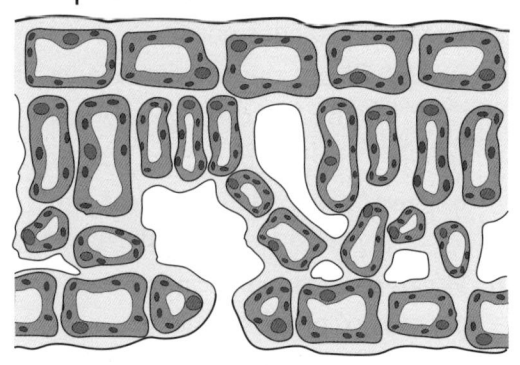

a Copy the diagram of a section through a leaf and add the labels below.

A palisade layer   D upper epidermis
B spongy layer   E chloroplast
C lower epidermis   F stoma

b Explain the function of each part in your labels.

28

23 Bigger and better crops

1 Copy and complete these sentences. Use the words below to fill in the gaps.

carbon dioxide   light   limit   oxygen photosynthesis   temperature

During .... a plant uses the energy from the sunlight to turn .... and water into glucose and .... This needs a plentiful supply of carbon dioxide and .... The .... is also important – it must not be too hot or too cold. If any of these conditions is not right it will .... the amount of photosynthesis that takes place.

2 The diagram shows the apparatus you would need to demonstrate photosynthesis in *Elodea* (pondweed).

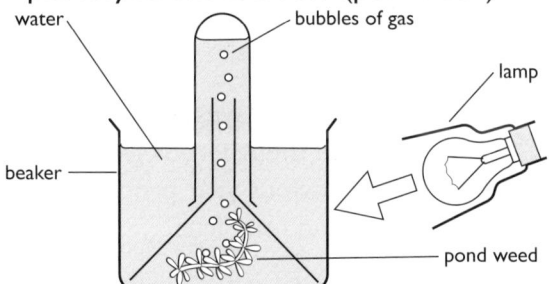

a How do you know when photosynthesis is actually taking place?
b You can use this basic apparatus to investigate the effect of light intensity on the rate of photosynthesis. What would you expect to happen if
  i you moved the light closer to the beaker containing the pondweed
  ii you moved the light further away from the pondweed?
c Why would you expect moving the light to have an effect on the rate of photosynthesis?
d Which other factor might be changing each time you move the lamp?

3 The table shows the mean growth of two sets of oak seedlings that were grown in different amounts of sunlight.

Year	Mean height of seedlings (cm) grown in 85% full sunlight	grown in 35% full sunlight
1966	12	10
1967	16	12.5
1968	18	14
1969	21	17
1970	28	20
1971	35	21
1972	36	23

a Plot a graph to show the growth of both sets of oak seedlings.
b Using what you know about photosynthesis and limiting factors, explain the difference in the growth of the two sets of seedlings.

4 The graph shows the effect of temperature on photosynthesis and respiration for a tomato plant.

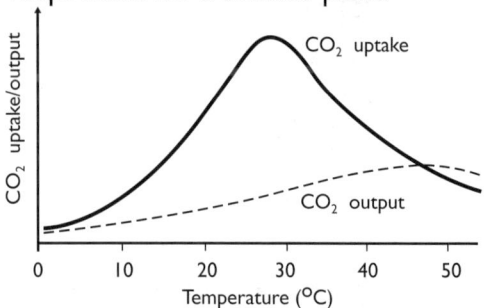

a At what temperature is photosynthesis in the tomato plant at a maximum?
b Describe the effect of temperature on the rate of photosynthesis in the tomato plant.
c At what temperature is respiration in the tomato plant at a maximum?
d To get the maximum yield of tomatoes, the plants need to be grown at their optimal temperature. This is the point at which the rate of photosynthesis exceeds the rate of respiration by the largest amount. Why will this result in the biggest crop of tomatoes?
e Which temperature will give the maximum yield from the tomato plants?

24 How does your garden grow?

1 Copy and complete these sentences. Use the words below to fill in the gaps.

cuttings   humid   light   nitrates propagator

When gardeners take .... they often put them in a special .... or even in a polythene bag. This gives the cuttings a warm, ... atmosphere. If they are also given plenty of .... and nutrients such as ...., they have ideal conditions for successful growth.

2 Read the passage and use it to help you answer the questions below. Answer using complete sentences.

Plants can make their own sugars by photosynthesis, but for healthy growth they need proteins and to make proteins they must have nitrogen.

Although there is a lot of nitrogen in the air, plants cannot use it. They need to absorb (take in) nitrates from the soil through their roots. These nitrates may be from the decaying bodies of animals and plants, or they may come from fertilisers added to the soil.

  a Why do plants need nitrates?
  b How do plants take in nitrates?
  c What are the possible sources of the nitrates in the soil?
  d If nitrates from fertilisers put on the soil find their way into rivers, they often lead to the rapid growth of algae and eventually the death of all living things in the river. Why does this happen?

3 Plants need certain nutrients to grow well.

Nutrients	Part played in the plant
magnesium (Mg)	• part of the chlorophyll molecule
nitrates (N)	• leaf and shoot production • produce amino acids (building blocks for proteins and enzymes)
phosphates (P)	• helps in the reactions of photosynthesis and respiration
potassium (K)	• good for flowers, fruit and disease resistance

At a plant clinic run by a fertiliser manufacturer, farmers turn up with plants which are not growing as well as they should. For each plant, explain what is wrong with it and suggest what needs to be done to the soil to make sure that crop growth improves.

Plant A has yellow leaves with dead brown spots on them. Crops grown in the field the previous year produced poor flowers and little fruit.

Plant B shows stunted growth, and the older leaves have turned pale and yellow.

Plant C has poor growth of both stems and roots. The young leaves show a purple colour whilst the older leaves are yellow.

Plant D has yellow leaves.

25 Watering holes

1 Copy and complete these sentences. Use the words below to fill in the gaps.

support   stomata   transpiration   waxy

Water inside plant cells provides the plant with .... Plants lose water vapour by evaporation through the .... (pores) in their leaves. This is known as .... Most plants have a waterproof .... layer on their leaves which stops them losing too much water.

2 Copy and label the diagram of a whole leaf and a leaf section. Use the labels below on your diagrams.

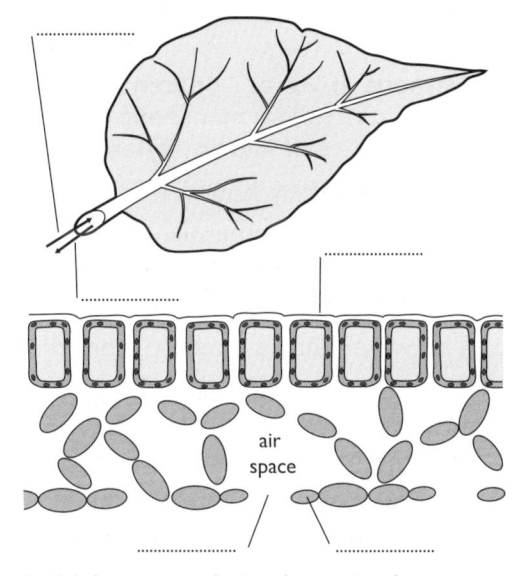

A Xylem vessels in the veins bring water to the leaves.
B Guard cells open and close the stomata, controlling water loss.
C The waxy cuticle on the top surface of the leaf helps reduces water loss.
D Phloem tubes in the veins carry sugars away from the leaf to all parts of the plant.
E Stomata allow carbon dioxide to diffuse into the leaf and water vapour to be lost by evaporation.

3 Copy and complete each sentence using the correct ending from below.
a Water loss by evaporation in a plant ...
b Transpiration is more rapid in ...
c Plants keep relatively cool in hot sun ...
d Transpiration also creates a risk ...

Choose endings from
- hot, dry and windy conditions.
- that the plant will lose too much water and wilt.
- because transpiration cools them down.
- is known as transpiration.

4 The diagram shows an experiment which is a model of osmosis in living cells.

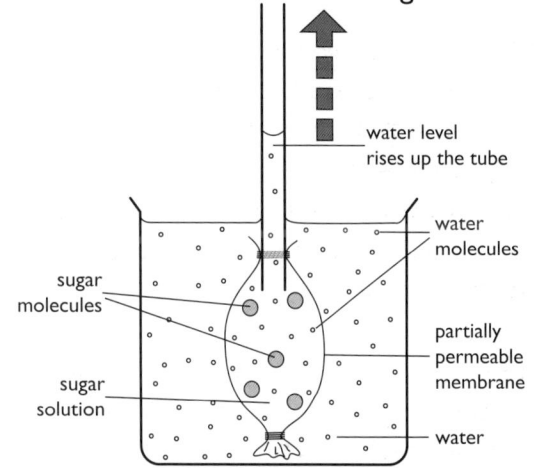

a Explain what is happening in the experiment.
b How is this model useful in explaining the entry of water into the xylem from the soil?
c Using your knowledge of osmosis and diffusion, explain why plants store all their excess carbohydrate as insoluble starch.
d Osmosis and diffusion take place along concentration gradients. When mineral ions such as nitrates are taken into plant roots they are often moved against a concentration gradient. What is this called?
e How does transpiration help in moving water up through the plant?
f Why is it an advantage for the roots to have a large surface area?

31

26 Absorbing roots

1 Plants make food in one organ and take up water from the soil in another organ. But both the food and the water are needed all over the plant.
   a Where do plants take in water?
   b There are two transport tissues in a plant. One is the phloem. What is the other?
   c Which transport tissue carries food around the plant?
   d Which transport tissue carries water through the plant?
   e What is the main difference between the cells of the two transport systems?

2 The diagram shows apparatus that can be used to give an idea of how much water a plant loses by transpiration. Use the diagram to help you answer the questions.

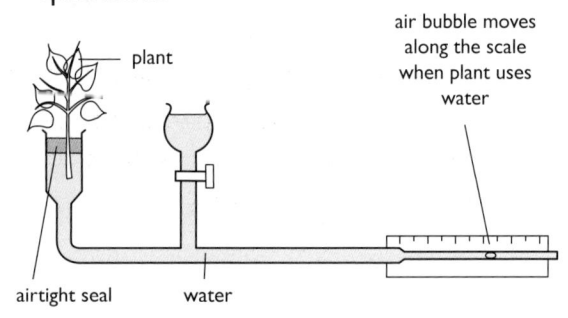

   a What is transpiration?
   b Which part of the leaves helps to prevent them from losing too much water under normal conditions?
   c If the top surfaces of the leaves were coated with Vaseline, how do you think it would affect the rate at which the plant takes up and loses water?
   d If the bottom surfaces of the leaves were coated in Vaseline, how do you think it would affect the rate at which the plant takes up and loses water?
   e What do you think would happen to the air bubble in the capillary tube if you turned a fan onto the leaves of the plant? Explain your answer.
   f What is the apparatus in the diagram actually measuring?

3 a Copy the diagram of a section through a root. Use the labels below to replace A–H on your diagram.

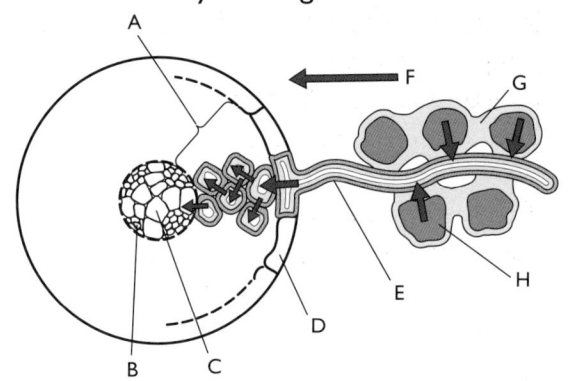

   movement of water   phloem   root cortex   root epidermis   root hair cell   soil particle   soil water   xylem

   b Explain carefully how water from the soil is taken into the plant and moved across to the transport tissue in the middle of the plant.
   c The water that is taken in from the soil is moved up through the whole plant. What process causes this movement of water?
   d Mineral ions are taken into the plants through the root hair cells as well as water. Explain carefully the difference between the uptake of water and the uptake of mineral ions in these cells.

4 a Explain carefully how transpiration results in a constant column of water moving through the plant from the roots to the leaves.
   b Describe a demonstration using a potometer which can be used to show how much water is taken up by a plant for use in transpiration. What are the limitations of this demonstration?

27 Plant growth responses

1 Copy and complete these sentences. Use the words below to fill in the gaps.
**hormones   gravity   growing
light   stimuli   tropisms**

Plants usually respond slowly to changes in their surroundings (called ....). They are sensitive to ...., moisture and the force of .... Plants respond by .... towards or away from a stimulus. The response is coordinated and controlled by .... produced by the plant. These responses are known as ....

2 Plant shoots and roots respond differently to stimuli. Copy these sentences, choosing the right word from each pair to describe how the plant responds.
   a Plant shoots grow **towards/away from** light. This is an example of **geotropism/phototropism**.
   b Plant shoots grow **towards/away from** gravity. This is an example of **geotropism/hydrotropism**.
   c Plant roots grow **towards/away from** moisture. This is an example of **phototropism/hydrotropism**.
   d Plant roots grow **towards/away from** gravity. This is an example of **hydrotropism/geotropism**.

3 The diagrams show shoot tips treated in different ways, and then exposed to bright light from one direction only.

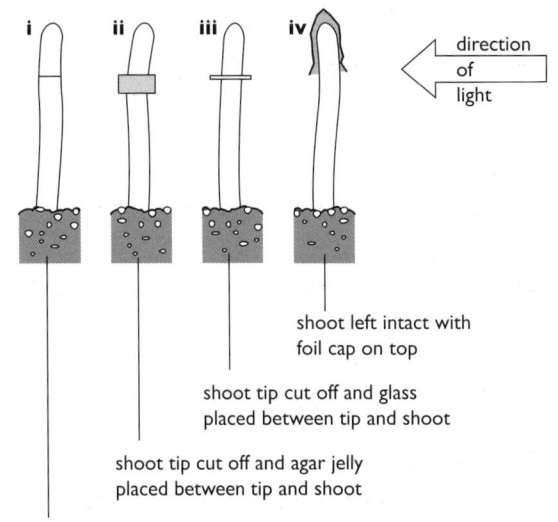

i   ii   iii   iv   ← direction of light

iv — shoot left intact with foil cap on top

iii — shoot tip cut off and glass placed between tip and shoot

ii — shoot tip cut off and agar jelly placed between tip and shoot

i — shoot tip cut off and replaced

   a Copy the diagrams. Under each diagram draw how you would expect it to look after two days.
   b Explain what has happened in each case.

The diagram below shows a shoot tip which has bent over in response to light from one side only.

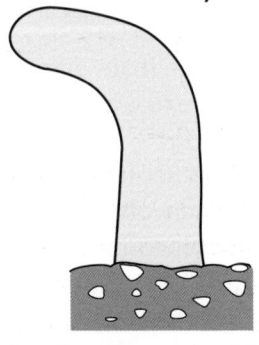

   c Copy the diagram and add arrows and labels to show
      i   the direction the light is coming from
      ii which side of the shoot has more of the hormone auxin.

28 Plant reproduction

1 Copy and complete these sentences. Use the words below to fill the gaps.

**asexually   brightly coloured
flowers   pollinated   scent
sexually   wind**

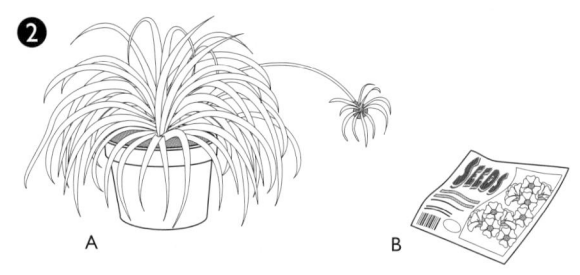

Plants reproduce .... and
.... contain
the sex organs of plants. They can be
.... by the ....
or by insects. Insect-pollinated flowers
are often .... and produce
.... and nectar.

2

a How has the baby plant in diagram A been produced?
b What sort of reproduction is this?
c How were the seeds in diagram B produced?
d How would the new plants grown from the packet of seeds differ from the baby plant in diagram A?

3 a What are the main differences between asexual and sexual reproduction?
b i Is the structure shown in the diagram involved in asexual or sexual reproduction in the plant?

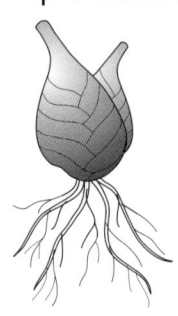

ii What is this reproductive structure called?
iii Explain how this structure is formed and its role in reproduction.

4 a Asexual reproduction is fairly common in plants. Explain how it takes place in these plants.
  i strawberries   ii potatoes
b Asexual reproduction can be used artificially by gardeners to reproduce particularly good plants. One method is by taking cuttings. Describe this process carefully and explain why it is a form of asexual reproduction.

5 a Copy and label this diagram of a flower.

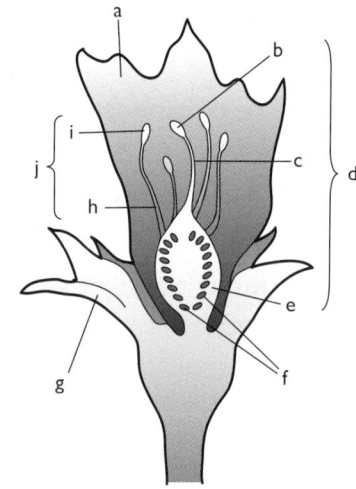

b What is meant by the term pollination?
c How do you think the flower in the diagram is pollinated? Explain your answer.

6 a Draw and label a typical wind-pollinated flower.
b Draw up a table with the following headings to show the main differences in the structure of an insect-pollinated flower and a wind-pollinated flower, and how the structures are related to their functions. You should include the position of the stamens, the position and type of stigma, the size and colour of petals, nectaries and pollen grains.

Feature of flower	Type of flower	
	Insect pollinated	Wind pollinated

29 Fertilisation and dispersal

1 a What is fertilisation?
b Look at the diagram of the fertilisation of a flower. Match the labels to the statements below to describe the sequence of events which lead to the fertilisation of a flower in the correct order.

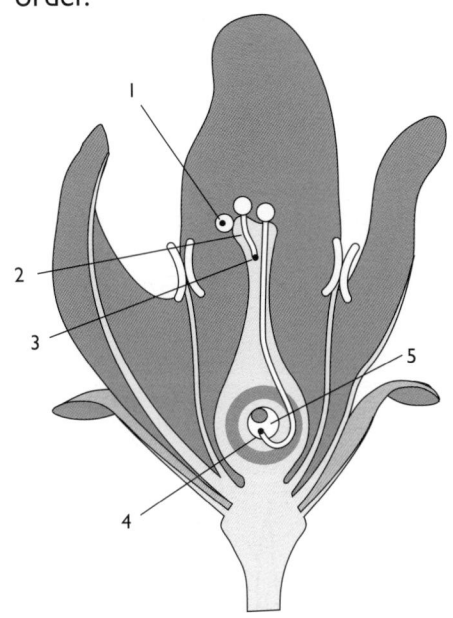

A The pollen grain (male) nucleus fuses with the egg nucleus.
B Pollen grains from another flower land on the stigma.
C The male nucleus moves to the tip of the tube.
D The pollen tube grows out of the pollen grain and down the style.
E The pollen tube penetrates the ovule.

2 a What is meant by the term 'dispersal of seeds'.
b Why is seed dispersal important to plants?
c How do you think each of the fruits in the diagram at the top right are dispersed? Explain your answers.

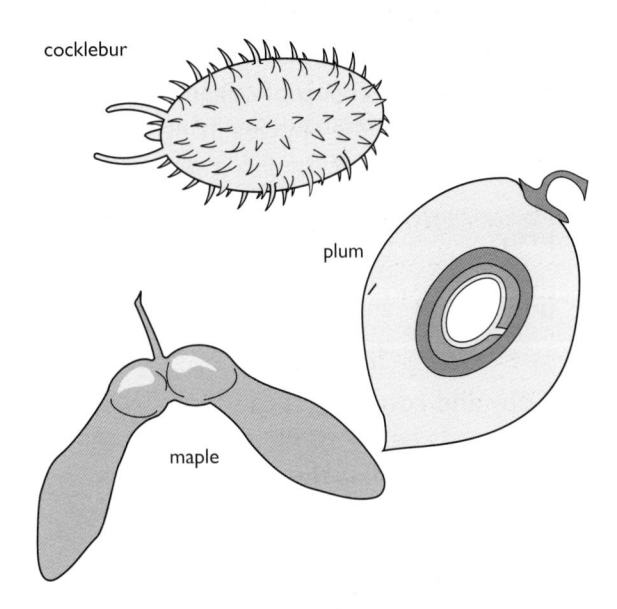

3 Inside a seed, what are
  a the cotyledons **b** the radicle
  c the plumule   **d** the testa?

4 a Describe three different ways in which plants can use the wind to disperse their seeds.
b Draw a series of labelled diagrams to show what happens when a seed germinates.

5 a What conditions do seeds need to germinate successfully and why?
b Choose one of these conditions and describe an investigation which you could use to demonstrate that this condition is needed for successful germination.

35

30 Community life

1 Match each words with its definition and copy them out.

community　a group of organisms of the same species living in an area
predators　all of the living organisms that share a habitat
prey　animals that kill and eat other animals
population　animals that are eaten by other animals

2 Copy and complete these sentences. Use the words below to fill in the gaps.

**animals　consumers　plants
primary consumers　producers
secondary consumers**

.... can make their own food using energy from the Sun so they are known as .... All of the .... in the community rely either directly or indirectly on the plants for their food – they are .... Animals that eat plants are called .... and animals which eat other animals are ....

3 The number of animals of one species is usually limited by the amount of food available.

Wrens are small birds that live in Britain all year round. They eat small insects and their larvae, spiders and a few small seeds. In 1963 there was a harsh winter, with snow and ice all over the country lasting for weeks. The graph at the top right shows the number of breeding pairs of wrens between 1962 and 1967.

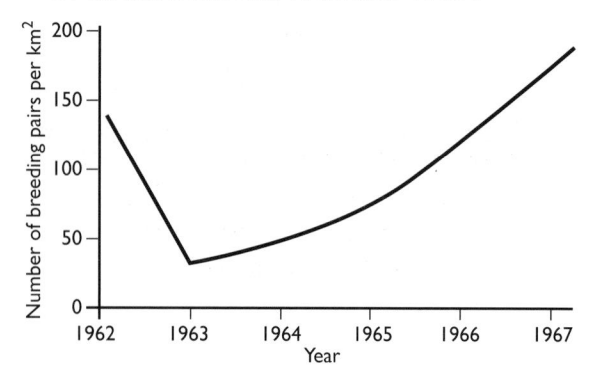

a How many breeding pairs of wrens per km^2 were there
　i in 1962　**ii** in 1963?
b Why do you think the wren population changed like this?
c How long did it take the wren population to recover?
d What do you think happened to the populations of insects which the wren eats in 1963 and 1964? Explain your answer.
e How might this have affected the recovery of the wren population?

4 Lynxes prey on snowshoe hares. The graph shows the number of snowshoe hares and lynxes in Canada between 1845 and 1885.

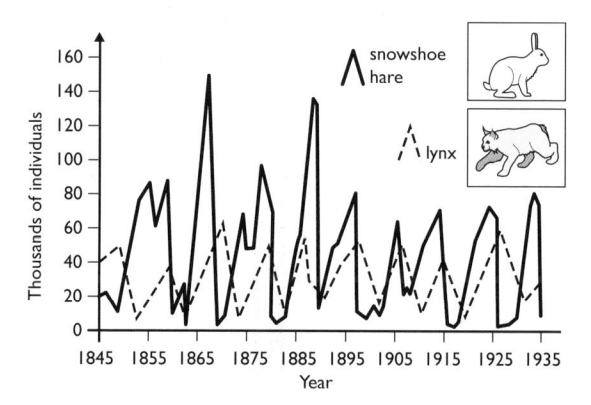

a What happens to the snowshoe hare population each time the lynx population peaks?
b Suggest why this happens.
c The data seem to show that the link between the two populations is very strong. However, other data on snowshoe hares in an area with no lynxes showed a very similar pattern of rise and fall. Suggest what else might cause these changes.

31 What is eating what?

1 Copy and complete these sentences. Use the words below to fill in the gaps.

**energy   photosynthesis   animals
food chains   producer**

All living things need .... Plants capture energy from the Sun and use it in .... to make food. Animals get their energy by eating plants or other ....
.... show us which organisms eat other organisms. They usually begin with a .... (green plant).

2 Here are five jumbled food chains. Sort each one into the right order and then write them down.

A stoat → primrose → rabbit

B water fleas → stickleback (small fish) → tiny water plants → pike (big fish)

C cow → grass → human

D tiny sea plants → seal → fish → polar bear

E blue tit → aphid → ladybird → rose bush

3 The diagram shows a food web from the Arctic tundra. Use it to help you answer the questions.

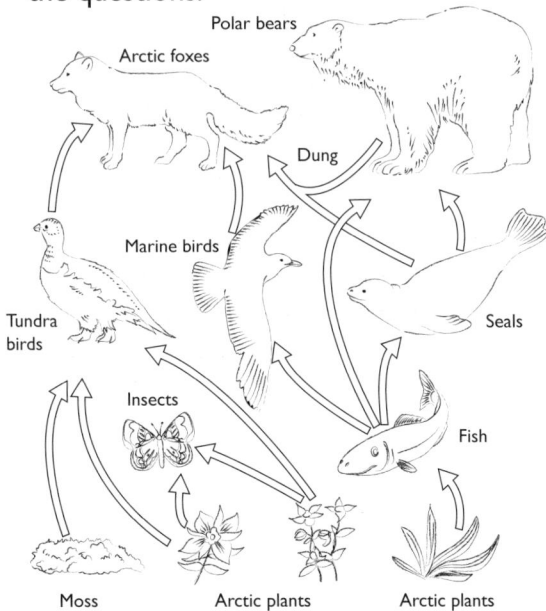

a Write down the producers in this system. Explain why they are important.

b Which organisms are the primary consumers?

c Which organisms are the secondary consumers?

d Draw three food chains which make up part of this web.

e Suggest what would happen to the other organisms if a new disease killed most of the seals?

f Why does a food web like this give a better picture of the real situation than a simple food chain would do?

4 Read the passage and use it to help you answer the questions.

The number of organisms at each stage of a food chain can be shown as a pyramid of numbers. The size of each block in the pyramid represents the number of organisms at that level.

a Draw a pyramid of numbers for these two food chains.
   i   clover → rabbit → fox
   ii tiny water plants → water fleas → stickleback

b Why are plants always at the base of the pyramid?

c Why are there fewer organisms at each level as you go up the pyramid?

5 a Draw the pyramid of numbers for this food chain.

rosebush → aphids → ladybirds → birds

b The diagram shows the same food chain as a pyramid of biomass. What is a pyramid of biomass?

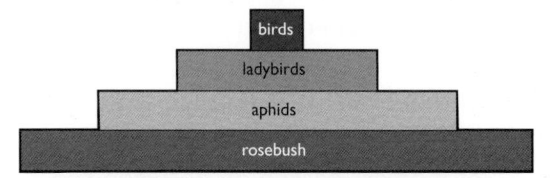

c Using the example in **a**, explain the advantages and disadvantages of
   i   pyramids of numbers
   ii pyramids of biomass.

32 Biomass and energy

1 At each stage of a food chain, there is less material and less energy in the biomass of the organisms.
  a Explain how the energy and biomass are used by the organisms in a food chain.
  b Explain what happens to the energy which is not transferred from one level to another.

2 The diagram shows a pyramid of biomass.

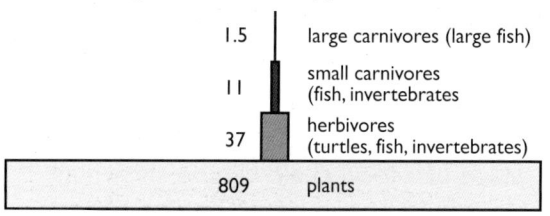

Value	Level
1.5	large carnivores (large fish)
11	small carnivores (fish, invertebrates)
37	herbivores (turtles, fish, invertebrates)
809	plants

(values give g dry biomass per m^2)

  a Calculate the percentage biomass passed on
   i from producers to primary consumers
   ii from primary to secondary consumers
   iii from secondary consumers to the top carnivores.
  b In any food chain or web, the biomass of the producers is much larger than that of any other level of the pyramid. Why is this?
  c In any food chain or web there are only a small number of top carnivores. Use your calculations to help you explain why.
  d All of the animals in the pyramid of biomass shown here are 'cold-blooded'. What difference would it have made to the average percentage of biomass passed on between the levels if 'warm-blooded' mammals and birds had been involved? Explain your answer.

3 Use the table to help you produce a leaflet either supporting intensive farming methods or supporting free-range farming methods. In each case back up your arguments with scientific reasoning.

Benefits	
Intensive farming	'Free-range' farming
• lots of chickens in small space	• chickens live more natural life
• little or no food wastage	• no heating/lighting costs
• energy wasted in movement/ heat loss kept to a minimum	• less food needs supplying as chickens find some for themselves
• maximum weight gain/ number of eggs laid	• can charge more money for free-range eggs/ chickens
• cheap eggs/chicken meat	
Costs	
Intensive farming	'Free-range' farming
• chickens unable to behave naturally, may be debeaked	• chickens more vulnerable to weather and predators
• large barns need heating and lighting	• more land needed for each bird
• chickens' legs may break as bones unable to carry weight of rapidly growing bodies	• eggs cannot be collected automatically
• risk of disease with many birds closely packed	

4 a What is a pyramid of energy transfer?
  b Why is a pyramid of energy transfer a more accurate way of representing what happens in feeding relationships than a pyramid of biomass?
  c Draw a typical pyramid of energy transfer and label each level carefully.

33 Removing nature's waste

❶ Copy and complete these sentences. Use the words below to fill in the gaps.

decomposed droppings leaves microorganisms nutrients recycled

Many trees shed their .... every year. Most animals produce .... at least once a day and all plants and animals eventually die. This dead plant and animal material is .... (broken down) by other organisms including .... As a result .... are returned to the soil and can be used again by plants. The same nutrients are .... again and again.

❷ Copy the diagram that shows how plants and animals are recycled by microorganisms. Use the labels below on your diagram.

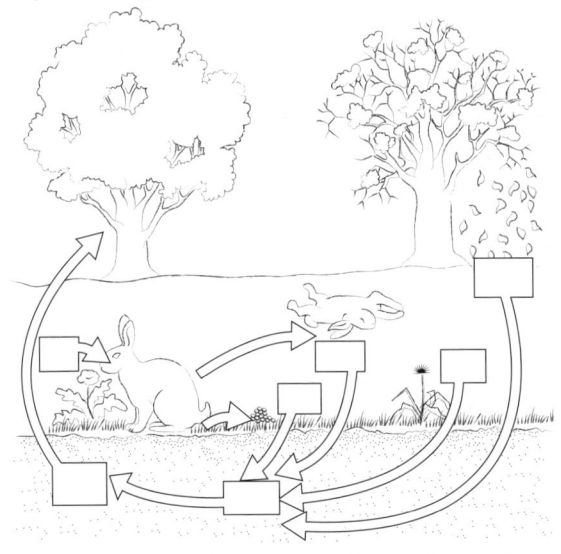

A Plants need nutrients from the soil to grow.
B Droppings, fallen leaves, dead animals and plants are broken down into simple chemicals by decomposers.
C Animals die.
D Animals produce droppings.
E Plants lose their leaves.
F Plants die.
G Animals eat plants.

❸ If farmers and gardeners let their crops rot down and ploughed them back into the soil, as in this diagram, the soil would stay full of nutrients and very fertile. The problem is there wouldn't be any food to eat!

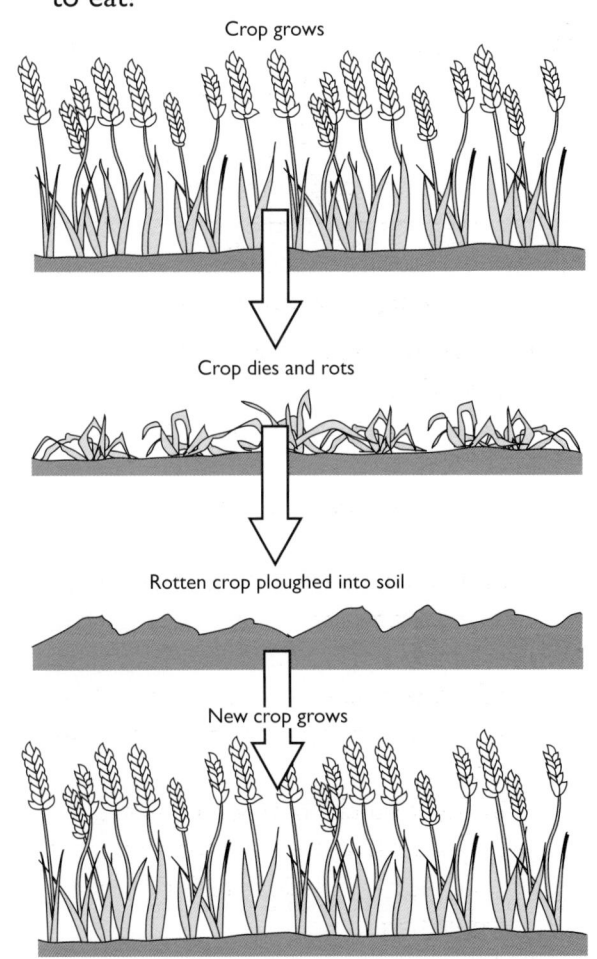

Crop grows

Crop dies and rots

Rotten crop ploughed into soil

New crop grows

Draw and label a diagram to show what really happens to the crops in a farmer's field, and how nutrients are replaced in the soil.

34 Chemical merry-go-round

❶ Copy and complete these sentences. Use the words below to fill in the gaps.
**carbon dioxide   decomposed
photosynthesise   respiration
waste product**

Plants and animals release energy from sugars in the process of .... They release carbon dioxide into the air as a .... When plants .... they use carbon dioxide from the air. When plants and animals die their bodies are .... by micoorganisms, releasing carbon dioxide into the air. When fuels like wood, coal, gas and petrol burn, they release carbon dioxide. So carbon in the form of .... is constantly being taken out of or put into the air.

❷ Oxygen and carbon dioxide are continuously produced and used in photosynthesis and respiration. Copy and complete the diagram to show how this happens.

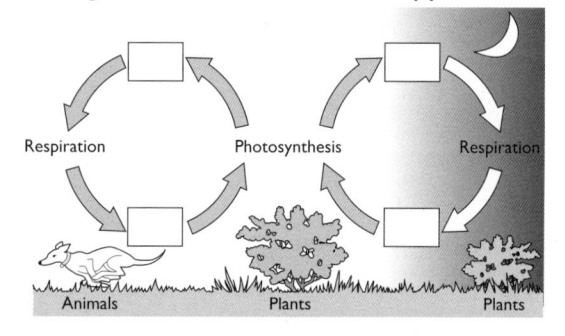

❸ Copy the diagram of the carbon cycle. Use the labels below on your diagram.

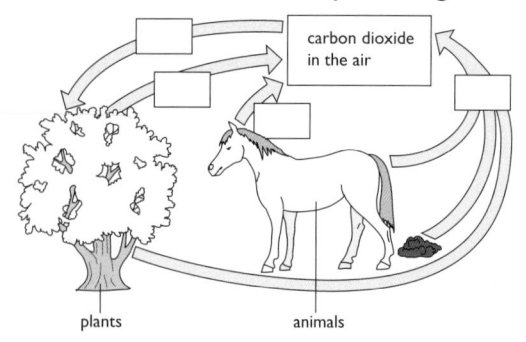

A Photosynthesis: plants remove carbon dioxide from the air and store the carbon in the food they make.
B Respiration: animals give off carbon dioxide as they release the energy from their food.
C Respiration: plants give off carbon dioxide as they release the energy from their food.
D Decay: carbon dioxide is released by microorganisms which decompose dead animals and plants and animals droppings.

❹ The graph shows the change in carbon dioxide levels in the atmosphere.
  a What happened to the levels of carbon dioxide in the atmosphere between 1960 and 2000?

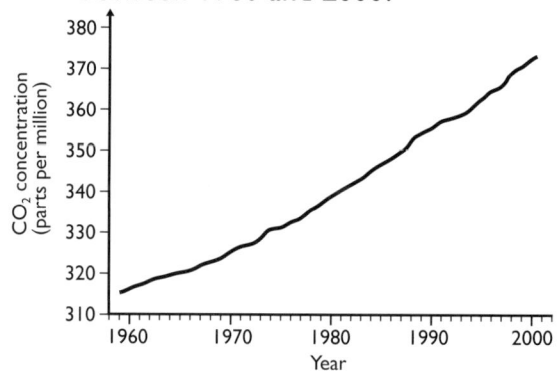

  b One possible cause of this effect is the increase in the amount of fossil fuels used by people. What is a fossil fuel?
  c What is produced when a fossil fuel burns?
  d Why has our use of fossil fuels increased so much?
  e Over the same period of time people have cut down enormous areas of forest. Why might this also have an effect on the levels of carbon dioxide in the air?

35 Nutrient cycles

1 a Why is nitrogen so important for living organisms?

b Some plants like beans and clover have special nodules on their roots which contain bacteria which can capture and 'fix' nitrogen from the air in a form which can be used by the plants. Why is this such an advantage for these plants?

2 Copy and label the diagram of the nitrogen cycle. Show clearly the role of microorganisms and detritus feeders in this cycle.

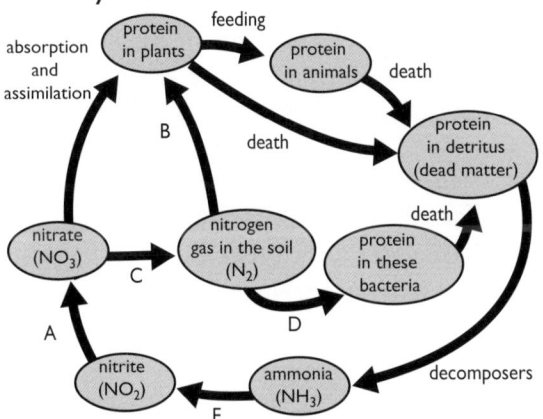

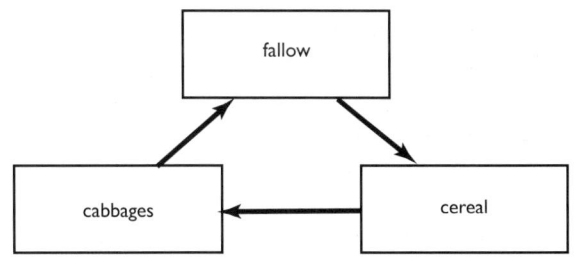

Using your knowledge of soil nutrients and the nitrogen cycle, explain why this crop rotation improved soil fertility. In particular, what was the importance of the fallow year?

4 The nitrogen cycle is vital in maintaining life. Answer the following questions carefully.

a Why is nitrogen such a key element in biological systems?

b What is the role of the following processes in the successful maintenance of the nitrogen cycle in nature?

  i feeding in heterotrophic organisms
  ii decomposition
  iii nitrogen fixing

3 One of the most important developments of the 18th century Agrarian Revolution in Britain was 'Turnip' Townsend's idea of three-field crop rotation.

His idea was that each field should be planted on a three-year rotation to improve crop yields. One year in every three the field should be rested (lie fallow), just planted with clover which should then be ploughed in. His idea proved very successful and people grew much more food as a result.

36 Life in the balance

1 Copy and complete these sentences. Use the words below to fill in the gaps.
**carbon dioxide   dissolved
photosynthesis   respiration   water**

Animals and plants which live in .... need oxygen and produce .... in the same way as organisms which live on the land. Pond animals and plants use oxygen .... in the pond water for .... As they respire they release carbon dioxide which dissolves in the water. This dissolved carbon dioxide is then used by water plants for ....

2 a Match each feeding group of organisms to the correct example, and then copy them out.

producers	animals like water boatmen and great diving beetles which eat other animals
herbivores	organisms like the waterlouse and various microorganisms which feed on decaying plant and animal remains
carnivores	green water plants which use the energy in sunlight to make food
decomposers	animals like the pond snail which feed on pond weed and other water plants

b Make a list of the organisms above which produce carbon dioxide.
c Make a list of the organisms above which use carbon dioxide.

3 A doctors' surgery installed a fish tank to liven up a dark corner of the waiting room. They put five fish and some water plants into the tank. However, they had a number of problems in keeping the fish alive. Explain what happened in each case.
  a The first five fish all died.
  b A light was put in the tank, and five more fish were added. These fish all survived.
  c One of the doctors brought another six fish and put them into the tank. Within a few days they started to die.
  d A patient brought in a small bubble pump which pumped air into the water and no more fish died, even when another fish was added.

4 a Why is water so important for life on Earth?
  b Copy this diagram of the water cycle and label it correctly.

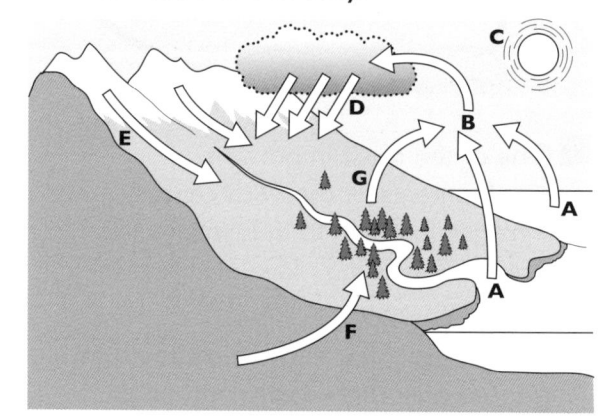

  c Explain carefully how the water cycle happens.
  d How do you think global warming might affect the water cycle?

37 Farming and pest control

1 Farmers need to control the environment so that they can get the maximum yield from their crops and livestock. Explain clearly how the following farming methods help to increase yields.
   a application of inorganic (artificial) fertiliser to the fields
   b application of farmyard manure (natural fertiliser) to the fields
   c growing a crop of leguminous plants
   d hydroponic systems

2 Copy and complete these sentences. Use the words below to fill in the gaps.
**biological   livestock   pesticides
pests   third   stored   yield**

.... are organisms which damage .... or crops and reduce the .... from a farm. Almost one .... of all the food grown in the world is lost to pests either in the fields or when the crop is .... Farmers use a variety of methods, including .... and .... control to try and prevent the damage.

3 a Many farmers use a range of chemicals to control pests. Draw up a table to show what the following chemicals are used for: molluscicide, herbicide, fungicide, insecticide.
   b What are the main advantages and disadvantages of using chemical pesticides?

4 a What is biological pest control?
   b What is the principle behind biological pest control?
   c Choose three of the following methods of biological pest control and explain how they work including an example: introducing a natural predator; introducing a herbivore; introducing a parasite; introducing a disease-causing microorganism; introducing sterile males; using pheromones.

5 Some time after DDT was introduced as a pesticide, people noticed that the number of large fish-eating birds like herons were falling. The tissues of these birds were analysed and found to contain amounts of DDT. The DDT made the birds produce eggs that had very thin shells which broke easily and killed the chicks inside. All of the animals in the food chain contained DDT, but only the large birds were affected like this.

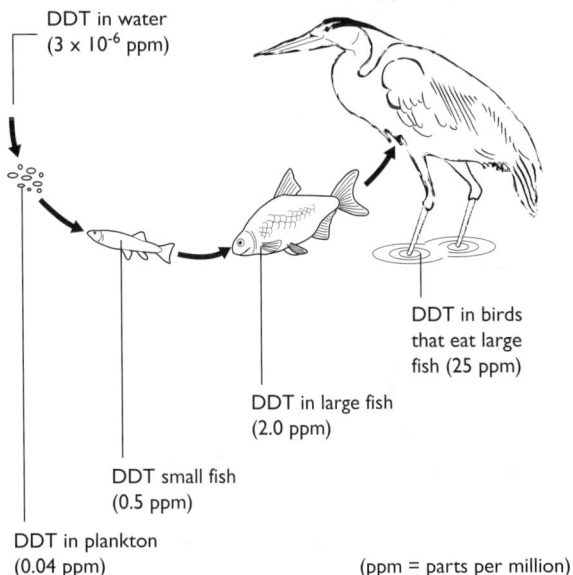

DDT in water (3×10^{-6} ppm)

DDT in birds that eat large fish (25 ppm)

DDT in large fish (2.0 ppm)

DDT small fish (0.5 ppm)

DDT in plankton (0.04 ppm)

(ppm = parts per million)

   a Explain how the levels of DDT increase in each level of the food chain.
   b When new pesticides are developed to be sprayed on our crops, what tests do you think should be carried out to make sure the chemical is safe?

38 Food production and forestry

1 A large scientific study published in the journal *Science* suggests that, unless we change our fishing habits, the world fish population will have completely collapsed within 50 years.

Global loss of seafood species

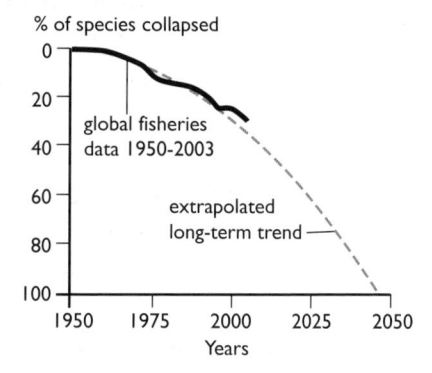

a What is meant by the term 'overfishing'?
b Using the graph, approximately when did the collapse in the number of fish species begin?
c When do scientists in this study think the seas will be fished out?
d What percentage of species will have collapsed by this year?
e Suggest two ways in which fish stocks might be protected.

2 One possible way of reducing the fall in fish stocks is fish farming.
a Name three species of fish that are commonly farmed.
b How are fish 'farmed'?
c What are the disadvantages of farming fish?

3 a Around the world there is an increasing awareness of the need for sustainable development. What do you think is meant by the term sustainable development?

In some areas of the world there are major problems with overgrazing.
b Explain what is meant by overgrazing.
c How does overgrazing cause environmental problems?
d Suggest solutions for the problems linked to overgrazing.

4 Look at the graph showing carbon dioxide concentration in the atmosphere.

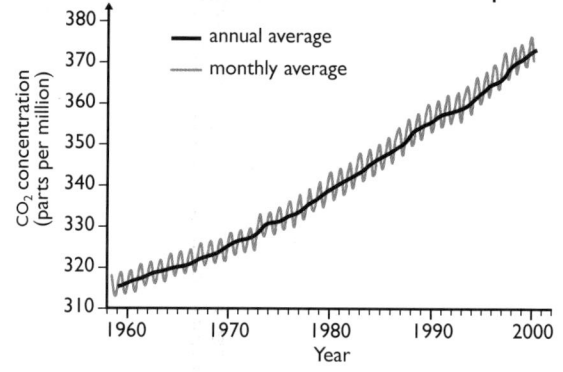

a What was the increase in concentration in carbon dioxide in the atmosphere between 1960 and 1990?
b Suggest as many sources as possible for this increase in carbon dioxide.
c The graph of carbon dioxide concentration shows regular peaks and troughs. Explain the cause of these.
d When large areas of forest are cut down this is known as deforestation. Explain the effects of this on the following.
  i soil erosion
  ii mineral leaching
  iii the water cycle
  iv the balance of oxygen and carbon dioxide in the atmosphere

39 A global threat

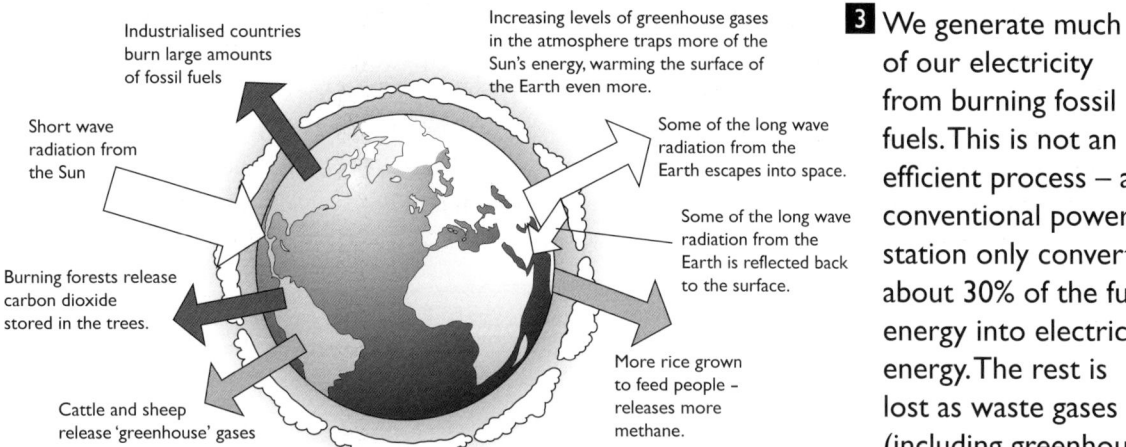

Industrialised countries burn large amounts of fossil fuels

Short wave radiation from the Sun

Burning forests release carbon dioxide stored in the trees.

Cattle and sheep release 'greenhouse' gases

Increasing levels of greenhouse gases in the atmosphere traps more of the Sun's energy, warming the surface of the Earth even more.

Some of the long wave radiation from the Earth escapes into space.

Some of the long wave radiation from the Earth is reflected back to the surface.

More rice grown to feed people – releases more methane.

❶ There are a number of gases in the atmosphere that play an important part in the greenhouse effect.
  a Write down three important greenhouse gases.
  b Explain why the greenhouse effect is important for life on Earth.

Increasing levels of some of these greenhouse gases have been measured over the last 50 years or so. Many scientists are concerned that this may be enhancing the greenhouse effect and causing global warming. Many say there is evidence that human activities are the cause of this warming. But not everyone agrees.
  c Using the information above along with any other information you may have, write an article for your local paper on the enhanced greenhouse effect to help ordinary people understand the issues. Explain what global warming is, how it may be caused and what it might mean for the future of the planet.

❷ Carbon monoxide is a colourless, odourless gas that pollutes the air.
  a Where does carbon monoxide in the atmosphere come from?
  b Why is it a dangerous air pollutant?

❸ We generate much of our electricity from burning fossil fuels. This is not an efficient process – a conventional power station only converts about 30% of the fuel energy into electrical energy. The rest is lost as waste gases (including greenhouse gases) and heat energy.

In some places Combined Heat and Power (CHP) stations have been built.

The waste heat produced in these power stations is used to provide hot water for heating and washing to all homes in the area. This results in an indirect reduction of greenhouse gas emissions from other sources that would be used to heat local homes.

CHP makes the power stations about 90% efficient, as much of the wasted heat energy is now used. In Woking, the local council has been able to reduce carbon dioxide production by 27% by introducing a CHP plant and by using electricity and other fuels carefully. Homes save up to £100 a year on their heating and electricity bills.
  a Explain how using waste heat from CHP can lead to an overall reduction in emission of greenhouse gases.
  b We can all affect greenhouse gas emissions on a small scale. Suggest as many ways as possible that you, your family and your school community might reduce your carbon footprint (in other words your carbon dioxide emissions).

40 Polluting the air

1 Copy and complete these sentences. Use the words below to fill in the gaps.
**acid rain   energy   fossil fuels
pollution   power stations
sulphur dioxide**

Burning .... causes air .... They release gases such as carbon monoxide, carbon dioxide, ... and nitrogen oxides. We burn fossil fuels in cars, ... and our homes and factories to produce .... These gases cause problems such as .... and global warming.

2 Copy and complete the diagram to show how acid rain is formed. Use the labels below on your diagram.

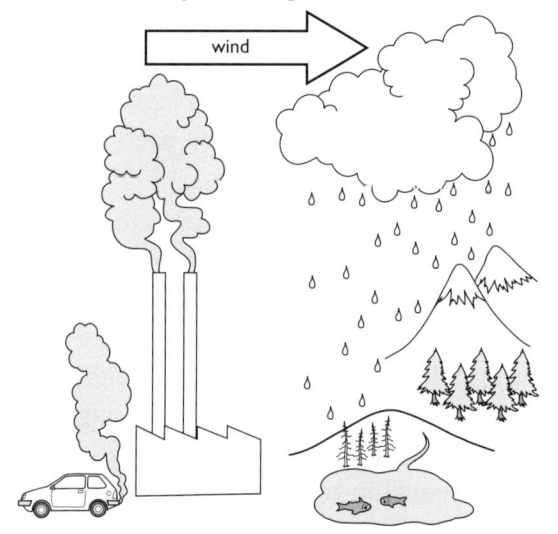

A Burning fossil fuels releases sulphur dioxide and nitrogen oxides.
B The gases blow in the wind to other areas or even other countries.
C The gases dissolve in rainwater and make it strongly acidic.
D Acid rain damages trees directly, killing the leaves and so the tree.
E Acid rain damages water life indirectly by making water in lakes and rivers more acidic – this kills plants and animals in the water.

3 In the late 20th century there were some severe problems of air pollution linked to the burning of fossil fuels. Here are some data that show the production of sulphur dioxide in some European countries in the late 1980s.

Country	Sulphur dioxide emitted (kg/person/year)
Hungary	153
Finland	119
Spain	99
Italy	90
Britain	83
Poland	76
Sweden	60
Netherlands	31
Switzerland	18

a Produce a bar chart to show the data more clearly.
b Which two countries were the highest producers of sulphur dioxide?
c Which two countries produced the least sulphur dioxide?
d Poland and Sweden were not the highest producers of sulphur dioxide, yet both countries have suffered enormous damage from acid rain. Explain how this could happen.
e Fossil fuels are still widely used, yet acid rain is no longer such a problem in European countries. Suggest how this problem has been dealt with.

4 The table shows the amount of some air pollutants in two areas.

| Air pollutant | Amount of air pollutant (µg per m³ air) | |
	area A	area B
sulphur dioxide	80	25
smoke	110	25
nitrogen dioxide	321	119
carbon monoxide	106	33

a Plot a bar graph to show the levels of air pollutants in area A and area B.
b Suggest where the pollutants might have come from.
c Why do you think the levels are so different in area A and area B?

41 Water pollution

1 Copy and complete these sentences. Use the words below to fill in the gaps.
**anoxic   eutrophication   oxygen
inorganic fertilisers   thermal
microorganisms   organic waste
power stations**

There are three main pollutants of fresh water: ...., ... and detergents. Fertilisers cause a problem known as .... where the water becomes ...., because .... use up all the oxygen. Other forms of water pollution include .... pollution, when warm water from .... reduces the amount of .... available in the water.

2 Use this information to answer the questions that follow.

Water pollution is a serious problem in many places around the world. One of the main pollutants is human sewage. In many of the countries much of the sewage – either raw or after it has been treated – is dumped into the water of rivers and seas. Sewage is biodegradable – it can be broken down and used as food by microorganisms like bacteria. Too much biodegradable material in the water can cause a serious problem of oxygen depletion in the water.

Sewage is broken down into harmless chemicals in water by aerobic bacteria which use oxygen dissolved in the water to break down their sewage 'food'. If there is plenty of sewage, the number of microorganisms will rapidly increase. If the numbers of aerobic bacteria get too high, they use up most of the dissolved oxygen. Other aquatic organisms which need oxygen, such as the fish, then die of suffocation. The dead fish provide more food for the decomposing microorganisms, so the problem gets worse until the water can no longer support life.

a What is meant by the term biodegradable?
b Suggest why the pollution of water by sewage is increasing around the world.
c Why does water pollution by sewage lead to an increase in the number of microorganisms in the water?
d What is meant by the term oxygen depletion and why does sewage pollution lead to oxygen depletion of the water?
e What effect does sewage pollution of the water supply have on other organisms such as fish and invertebrates in the water?

3 The graph shows what happened to the nitrate and oxygen levels in a stream close to a large arable farm after a wet spring.

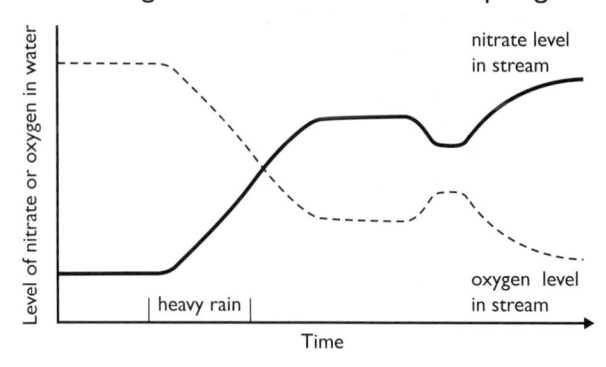

a Why did the nitrate levels in the stream rise so noticeably?
b What would you expect to happen to the plant population of the stream as a result of this rise?
c How would you explain the dip in the nitrate level followed by another rise?
d What would you expect to happen to the microorganism population of the stream?
e How is this related to the change in the oxygen level in the water?
f What effect would these changes have on the fish population of the stream?
g What is this type of pollution called?
h Why would it be very difficult to find out who was to blame for the pollution?

42 Similarities and differences

1 Copy and complete these sentences. Use the words below to fill in the gaps.
**characteristics   chromosomes
genes   offspring   parents**

Young animals and plants look like their .... They have similar characteristics because of information passed on from parents to .... in the sex cells from which they have developed. The information is carried by the .... which make up the .... found in the nucleus of every cell. Different genes control the development of different ....

2 Match the words to the part they play in reproduction. Copy out the correct pairs.

nucleus	contains the chromosomes which carry genes from the father
sperm	contains the chromosomes carrying thousands of genes
egg	contains chromosomes from both parents
fertilised egg	contains the chromosomes which carry genes from the mother

3 a What do the initials DNA stand for?
  b What is a gene?
  c The bases in DNA are adenine, guanine, thymine and cytosine. How do these bases pair up in the complementary strands of DNA?

4 a Describe the structure of a DNA molecule.
  b Explain why you can work out the sequence of the bases on one strand by looking at the sequence on the other.
  c Here is part of a strand of DNA. Write down the sequence of its complementary strand:
  ATGTTTACCGATGGGAACTGA.
  d What do we mean by the term 'triplet code'?
  e Use the table at the bottom of the page to work out the amino acid sequence that the DNA strand in part **c** codes for.

TTT phenylalanine
TTC phenylalanine
TTA leucine
TTG leucine	CTT leucine
CTC leucine
CTA leucine
CTG leucine	ATT isoleucine
ATC isoleucine
ATA isoleucine
ATG methionine/ start	GTT valine
GTC valine
GTA valine
GTG valine
TCT serine
TCC serine
TCA serine
TCG serine	CCT proline
CCC proline
CCA proline
CCG proline	ACT threonine
ACC threonine
ACA threonine
ACG threonine	GCT alanine
GCC alanine
GCA alanine
GCG alanine
TAT tyrosine
TAC tyrosine
TAA stop
TAG stop	CAT histidine
CAC histidine
CAA glutamine
CAG glutamine	AAT asparagine
AAC asparagine
AAA lysine
AAG lysine	GAT aspartic acid
GAC aspartic acid
GAA glutamic acid
GAG glutamic acid
TGT cysteine
TGC cysteine
TGA stop
TGG tryptophan	CGT arginine
CGC arginine
CGA arginine
CGG arginine	AGT serine
AGC serine
AGA arginine
AGG arginine	GGT glycine
GGC glycine
GGA glycine
GGG glycine

43 Mutation

1 Copy and complete these sentences. Use the words below to fill in the gaps.

genes   mutagens   variation   radiation   mutations

New forms of genes arise from changes known as .... in the existing .... These occur naturally and are important for producing .... The chance of mutations occurring is increased by exposure to ionising .... and chemicals known ....

2 Ionising radiation can come from radioactive substances such as uranium, ultraviolet light from the Sun and X-rays.
  a When you need to have an X-ray, the parts of your body which are not being X-rayed are covered in lead which absorbs radiation. Explain why.
  b People who work in X-ray departments move into a radiation-proof cubicle when operating the X-ray machine. The levels of radiation they receive are carefully monitored. Why is so much care taken with people who work with ionising radiation?

3 Cigarette smoke contains a number of carcinogens. These are mutagens that make cells develop in an uncontrolled way.

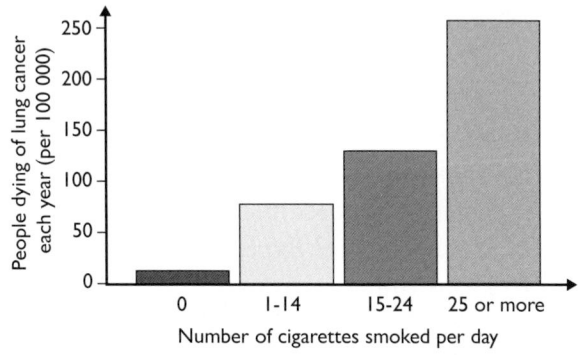

  a What effect does smoking cigarettes have on your chance of dying from lung cancer?
  b What effect does smoking cigarettes have on the levels of mutagenic chemicals in your body?
  c Why does smoking have a particular effect on the incidence of lung cancer?

4 The table shows the effect of an increasing radiation dose on the number of mutations found in cells.

Radiation dose (grays)	Number of mutations per 100 cells
0.05	1
0.1	2
0.25	6
0.5	11
0.75	18
1.1	28
1.35	32

  a Plot a graph of these results, drawing a line of best fit through the points.
  b What does your graph show you about the effect of increasing doses of radiation on the rate at which mutations occur?

5 Low doses of radiation may cause mutations to occur in any cells of the body. Explain carefully the long-term implications of
  a mutations in the reproductive cells
  b mutations in normal body cells.

6 Random mutations may cause small changes in the way the body develops and works. The graphs show how the numbers of resistant insects in a population changed with application of pesticide.

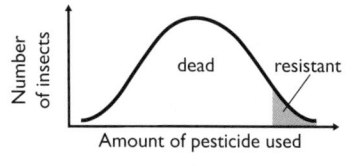

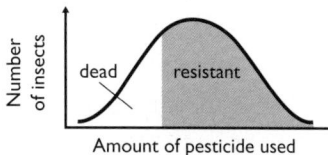

Explain how a pesticide can become ineffective against a type of insects as a result of mutations.

44 Division and inheritance

1 When gametes fuse at fertilisation, they form a single cell. This cell divides to produce millions of cells with an exact copy of the chromosomes to form a baby. This cell division is called mitosis.

  a Copy and complete the diagram to show how mitosis happens. You will need to add chromosomes, labels and arrows.

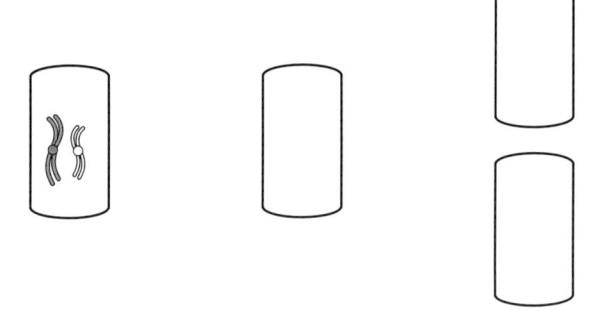

  b Why is it important that exact copies of the chromosomes are made?

  c Mitosis is also important all through your life. Explain why.

2 Explain the roles of the different types of cell division in
  a human reproduction
  b the production of new plants from cuttings.

3 a How many chromosomes are there in a normal human body cell?
  b How many chromosomes are there in a human gamete (sex cell)?
  c What is the name of the special type of cell division which produces gametes from normal cells?
  d Whereabouts in the body would this type of cell division take place?
  e The diagram shows this type of cell division. Copy and label it to explain what is happening at each stage.

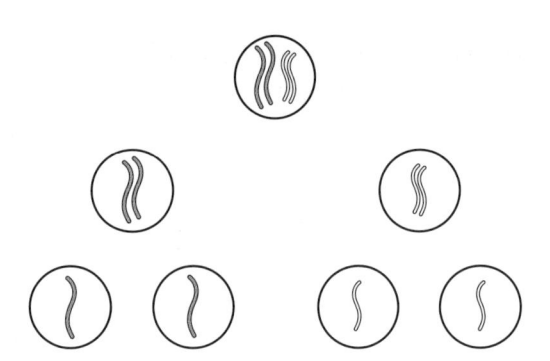

4 Sometimes identical twins are separated at birth, adopted and brought up in different families. Comparing these genetically identical individuals who have been brought up in different environments with other identical twins brought up together gives us some useful information. We can then compare this with non-identical twins and ordinary brothers and sisters.

Characteristic	Identical twins brought up together	Identical twins brought up apart	Non-identical twins	Non-twin siblings
height difference (cm)	1.7	1.8	4.4	4.5
mass difference (kg)	1.9	4.5	4.6	4.7

  a Draw bar graphs to show these data clearly.
  b Which feature, height or mass, do you think is least affected by the environment identical twins are brought up in? Explain your answer.
  c Does the comparison made with non-identical twins and ordinary siblings confirm your answer to part **b**? Explain your answer.
  d This type of data on identical twins is very useful but quite rare. Why do you think such information is difficult to collect?

50

45 Patterns of inheritance

❶ Match each word with its definition and then copy them out.

gene	when both chromosomes in a pair contain different alleles of a gene
allele	allele that controls the development of a characteristic only when present on both of a pair of chromosomes
dominant allele	when both chromosomes in a pair contain the same allele of a gene
recessive allele	different form of a gene
homozygous	unit of genetic information linked to a particular characteristic
heterozygous	allele which controls the development of a characteristic when present on only one of a pair of chromosomes

❷ Whether you can roll your tongue or not is possibly decided by a single gene with two alleles. The 'roller' allele **R** is dominant to the 'non-roller' allele **r**. Use this information to help you answer these questions.

Tom can roll his tongue but Sandy can't. They are expecting a baby.
 a What are Sandy's tongue-rolling genes? How do you know?
 b If the baby develops to be unable to roll its tongue, what does this tell us about Tom's tongue-rolling genes?
 c If the baby develops to be a tongue roller, what does this tell us about Tom's tongue-rolling genes?

❸ Manx cats are born with no tail. If a Manx cat is mated to a normal cat, half the litter will have tails and half will not. This suggests that Manx cats are heterozygous for a dominant gene **T**, which causes no tail to form, with the normal tail gene **t** being recessive.
 a Show the Manx cat cross described above.

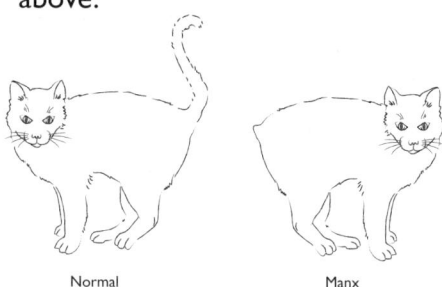

Normal   Manx

However, when two Manx cats are mated there are always fewer Manx kittens born than we would expect. The homozygous form of the **T** gene is so damaging that the kittens which are homozygous for **T** die before birth.
 b Show a cross between two Manx cats. What ratio of Manx kittens to normal kittens would you expect to be born if the homozygous form was not so damaging?
 c What ratio of Manx kittens to normal kittens is actually born, and why?

❹ The sex of a new human being is decided at the moment of conception.
 a Draw a genetic diagram to show how sex is determined in humans.

The cells in some people show a dark patch inside the cells known as the Barr body. This shows that one of their two X chromosomes has been deactivated.

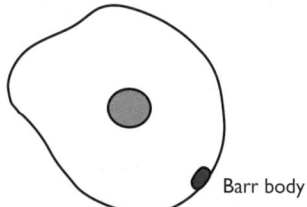

Barr body

 b A group of young people were tested for the presence of a Barr body. 20 showed the Barr bodies and 24 did not.
   i How many of those tested were men?
   ii How can you tell?

46 Genetic problems

1 Peas are usually round and smooth, but sometimes they are wrinkled. One gene controls this with two alleles, round and wrinkled. The round allele **W** is dominant to the wrinkled allele **w**.

A gardener has been given a pea plant with round peas. Before breeding it with a pure-breeding plant that has round peas, she wants to check the plant is not heterozygous for the wrinkled gene by crossing it with a pure-breeding wrinkled plant.

Show the cross and the results they would get if the gardener's peas were
  a homozygous
  b heterozygous for the round allele.

2 Cystic fibrosis is a genetic disease which particularly affects the lungs and the gut. It is carried on a recessive allele. Frankie and Annie are planning a family. Frankie's sister has cystic fibrosis, and tests have shown that he is a carrier. Annie has had tests too, and she is not a carrier of the faulty allele.
  a Choose a suitable capital and lower-case letter to represent the normal and cystic fibrosis alleles. Produce a genetic diagram to show the chance of Annie and Frankie having a child affected by cystic fibrosis.
  b Steve and Paula also want to start a family. Neither of them has any cystic fibrosis in their families, but this does not guarantee they are not carriers. Produce genetic diagrams to show the different possibilities of them producing a child suffering from cystic fibrosis.

3 Achondroplastic dwarfism is a genetic condition which affects the long bones of the body which do not grow to normal size, although in every other way affected individuals are quite normal. It is inherited as a dominant gene. Embryos which are homozygous for achondroplastic dwarfism die before birth. Use this family tree to help you answer the following questions.

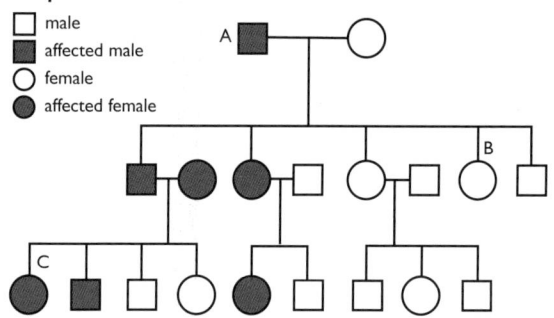

□ male
■ affected male
○ female
● affected female

  a Choose a suitable capital and lower-case letter to represent the two alleles. Give the genotype you would expect for individuals A, B and C in the family tree.
  b In the family where two people with achondroplastic dwarfism married, one pregnancy ended in miscarriage. What might be the explanation for this? Use a genetic diagram to help you explain.

47 Natural selection in action

1 Ptarmigans are birds, members of the grouse family, which are found in Scotland. Their summer plumage is a mixture of browns and cream, but after the autumn moult the feathers of most of the birds grow back almost white. A relatively small number of ptarmigans keep their normal brown-and-cream colouring.
  a How is it possible for the winter plumage of different members of the same species of bird to be so different?
  b Is there likely to be a disadvantage in having brown feathers during a Scottish winter?
  c Do you think that having white feathers in the winter increases the breeding chances of those ptarmigans which change colour?
  d Does the fact that the majority of ptarmigan have white plumage in winter confirm your hypothesis?

2 In 1915 oyster fishermen in Malpeque Bay in Canada noticed a few of the oysters they caught were diseased. They were small and had pus-filled blisters. The graph shows the effect of this disease on the oyster population in that area.

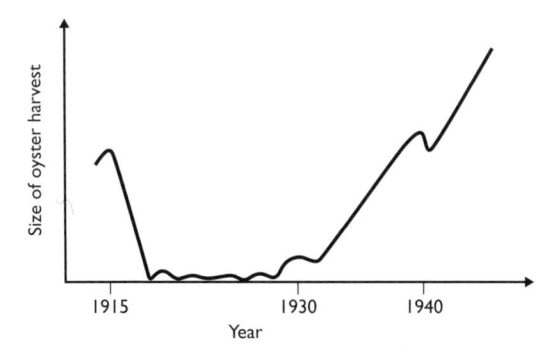

  a How long did it take for the oyster harvest to be virtually wiped out?
  b In which year did the harvest really start to pick up again?
  c How long was it before the oyster numbers returned to their 1914 numbers?
  d Explain what happened in Malpeque Bay in terms of natural selection.

3 The finches that Charles Darwin studied on the Galapagos Islands were some of the organisms which led him towards the idea of natural selection as the force behind evolution. On the mainland there is only one type of finch. Yet on the tiny Galapagos Islands there are six main types of finch and 13 separate species. They live on different islands or on different parts of the same island. Different species have different shapes of beak which helps them specialise on feeding on different foods, such as fruit, seeds, nectar and insect larvae. Use the theory of natural selection to explain carefully how this variety might have come about.

4 a What is sickle cell disease?
  b Two people who are heterozygous for sickle cell disease have four children, one of whom has severe sickle cell disease, one who is quite normal and two who have mild anaemia. Produce a genetic diagram to show this cross.
  c People who are heterozygous for sickle cell disease have a greatly improved immunity to malaria, a tropical disease which kills about two million people a year in the developing world. How does this affect which of the children in the family above is/are most likely to live to adulthood
    i if the family live in Africa
    ii if the family live in the UK?
  Explain your answers.

48 Selecting the best

❶ Copy and complete these sentences. Use the words below to fill in the gaps.
characteristics   cuttings   identical   parents

New plants can be produced quickly and cheaply by taking .... from older plants. These new plants are genetically .... to their .... This means if cuttings are taken from a plant that has the .... you want, all the cuttings will have them as well.

❷ We develop new varieties of animals and plants by choosing individuals which have useful characteristics and breeding from them. The new variety may end up looking very different from the original parent. For example, the wheat we use for flour has been developed over thousands of years from wild grasses.
  a What do we call breeding animals and plants to get the characteristics we want?
  b Copy and complete this table of animals and plants which have been selectively bred for particular reasons.

Animal selected	Reason why
hens from wild chickens	i
pigs from wild boar	ii
iii	large milk production
dogs from wolves	iv
Plant selected	**Reason why**
wheat from wild grasses	large 'ears' for food
potatoes from wild potatoes	v
vi	larger, sweeter fruit
garden roses from wild roses	vii

❸ The graph shows the increase in world population over the last 10 000 years.

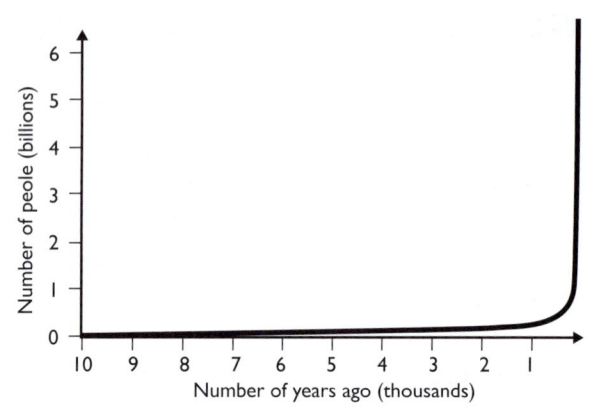

  a Describe the shape of the graph.
  b Why is it important to increase the yields of many of our crops?

Many scientists are working hard to develop plants which not only give more and more crops but which are also resistant to disease. The table shows the percentage of the total crops lost to disease and pests between 1988 and 1990.

Crop	% loss
Wheat	32
Maize	38
Potatoes	40
Vegetables	50
Citrus fruits	31

  c Draw a bar chart to show this data more clearly.
  d Which crops were most affected by pests and disease?
  e Why is resistance to disease as important as increased yields of crops?

❹ a Selective breeding has developed cows which can produce more and more milk. What do you think is the advantage of this?
  b Suggest any disadvantages.
  c How could you increase the meat yield of an animal like a pig?

49 High technology breeding

1. Large numbers of identical plants can be grown using micropropagation.
   a How does tissue culture differ from traditional methods of taking cuttings?
   b Write down the advantages of micropropagation over traditional methods of propagation by cuttings.
   c Although there are many advantages to these modern techniques, there is also a great disadvantage which is that plants species propagated like this may not survive any major changes in conditions. Why is this?

2. Cloning is no longer a technique used only on plants. Animal clones are now possible too. The arrival of Dolly, the first cloned sheep, caused a considerable stir and the technique continues to be used. Many of the sheep that are cloned are transgenic – they have been genetically modified to produce human proteins. Produce a flow diagram to show the stages in cloning a sheep.

3. a What is the difference between selective breeding and genetic manipulation?
   b Cloning is particularly useful when a genetically modified parent animal or plant is involved. Why is this the case?
   c Some people are very worried about cloning. Give one possible problem which could arise.

4. Micropropagation techniques mean that we can produce thousands of new plants from one old one, whereas we would get only a few new plants from one parent by taking cuttings. Extracting and cloning embryos from the best cows means that they can be genetically responsible for hundreds of calves each year instead of simply two or three at most.

   a What are the similarities between cloning plants and cloning animals in this way?
   b What are the differences in the techniques for cloning animals and plants?
   c Why is there so much interest in finding different ways to make the breeding of farm animals and plants increasingly efficient?

50 Using microorganisms

1 a List as many things made using microorganisms as you can think of.
 b i Compare the structure of a yeast with that of a mould.
  ii Why do you think they are both classified as fungi?
 c Compare the structure of moulds and yeasts with those of bacteria and viruses. In what ways are they similar and how do they differ?

2 Write word equations to show the difference between aerobic and anaerobic respiration in yeast.

3 Draw a flow chart to explain the process of making beer.

4 a Temperature is vital for successful beer and wine making. Explain why it is so important.
 b Sometimes a small amount of yeast is left in a bottle of wine to make sparkling wine or champagne.
  i Explain why the yeast is left in the bottle.
  ii What is the gas which makes the bubbles in the drink?

5 Draw a flow chart to summarise the production of yoghurt from milk.

6 a Give as many reasons as you can why microorganisms are so useful in industrial processes.
 b Use this diagram to help you explain how an industrial fermenter is adapted to ensure the best possible conditions for the growth of a particular microorganism.

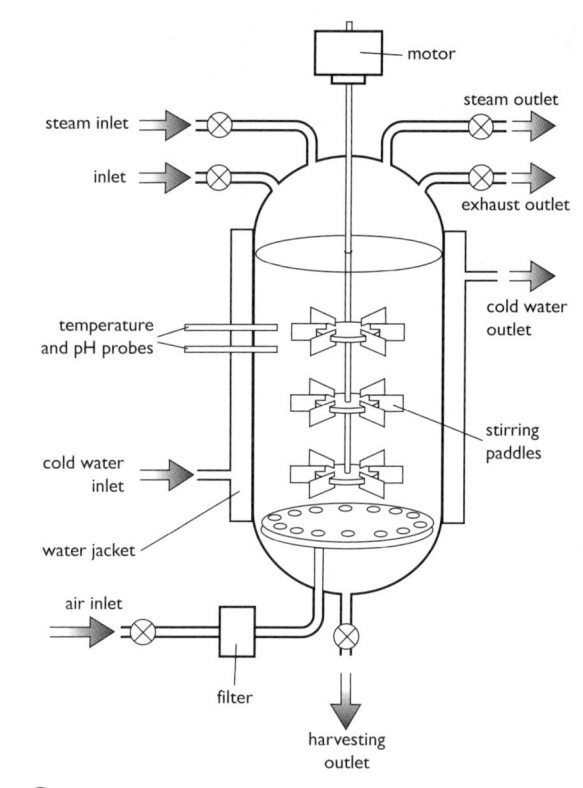

7 Why do the following factors tend to change during a fermentation process?
 a temperature
 b oxygen
 c pH

8 Produce a flow chart for the production of penicillin in a commercial fermentation process.

51 Genetic modification

1 a Give three advantages of genetic modification and explain how they benefit people now or may do in the future.
  b Choose three disadvantages of genetic modification and explain why some people are so strongly against it.

2 There are hopes that genetically modified plants can play a big part in preventing malnutrition around the world by improving food production. Explain carefully how this might work.

3 Human growth is usually controlled by the pituitary gland in the brain. If the pituitary gland does not make enough hormone, a child does not grow properly and remains very small. This condition affects 1 in every 5000 children.

Until recently the only way to overcome this condition was to extract growth hormone from the pituitary glands of dead bodies, but it took many bodies to produce enough hormone to enable one child to grow properly.

Genetic modification means that pure growth hormone can now be produced in relatively large amounts by bacteria.
  a Copy and label the diagram to explain how a healthy human gene for making growth hormone can be taken from a human chromosome and inserted into a working bacterial cell.
  b What are the advantages of producing substances such as growth hormone using genetic modification?

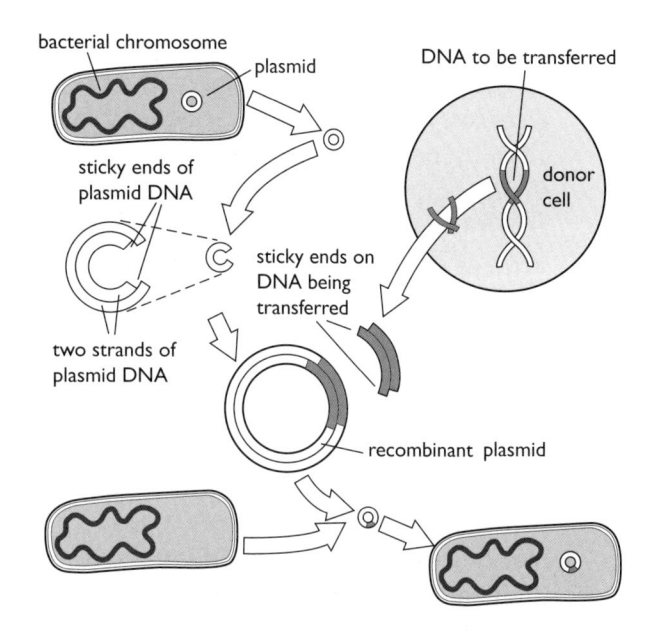

4 a What is the role of insulin in the body?
  b Genetic modification has made it possible for microorganisms to produce human insulin. In which ways is human insulin from microorganisms better for people with diabetes than insulin from animals?

5 The process of genetic modification in plants differs in some ways from that in animals. Explain carefully the process of genetically modifying plants using *Agrobacterium*. Describe the role of restriction enzymes and ligase enzymes in the process.

52 Biotechnology

1 Biotechnology is changing the way we can produce food and drugs, and treat diseases. This can be a great benefit to all of us, but there are issues we need to think about. Here are some comments about the uses of biotechnology.

A human gene for the production of a useful protein can be transferred into an animal such as a sheep or a cow. When that animal lactates (produces milk) the human protein is present in the milk and can easily be extracted and purified. One example is a human blood-clotting factor which can be given to people whose blood does not clot properly without them running any health risks from the blood of other people.

My son is really short, but there's nothing wrong with him. Tall people always seem to get more respect and better jobs – I want my son to be given some of this new growth hormone stuff they're getting from bacteria so he can end up 1.8 m tall instead of only 1.6 m!

Now growth hormone can be produced in relatively large amounts using genetically engineered bacteria, there is a growing 'black market' for the drug as some athletes and body builders want to buy it. In adults the hormone may help to increase muscle growth. As one athlete said 'Growth hormone occurs naturally in your body, so it will be really difficult for the dope testers to pick it up. It could be the performance-enhancing drug of the future.'

  a Using the information given here and any ideas of your own, list some of the advantages from advances in biotechnology.

  b Growth hormone is produced to help children whose bodies do not naturally make enough of the hormone.
    i Why do you think that parents with short or even average-height children might be prepared to pay for growth hormone treatment?
    ii Explain why some athletes want to buy the hormone.
    iii Do you think that either of these uses should be allowed? Give reasons for your answer.

  c Write a letter to your local newspaper either supporting or objecting to the introduction and use of new biotechnology. Whichever viewpoint you take, support your arguments with facts as far as possible.

2 Scientists are using genetic engineering techniques to breed pigs with special human proteins on their hearts and kidneys so their organs can be used for human transplants without any fear of the new heart or kidney being rejected. Some people find this idea objectionable, or worry about the risk of transferring diseases across the species, but doctors say that donor organs from people are in such short supply they have to look at other possibilities.

Most people are happy to accept the benefits of using engineered bacteria to produce human proteins. More people have concerns about putting human genes into animals like cows, pigs and sheep. Many people are very unhappy at the idea of transplanting organs from an animal such as a pig into a person, even if they are genetically 'human'.

  a Why do you think people are less concerned about products from bacteria than those formed using sheep and cows?

  b What are the advantages and disadvantages of using organs from other animals in human transplants? Can you think of any other way the shortage of suitable donor organs might be dealt with?

Glossary

acid rain	Rain containing dissolved gases from burning fossil fuels which make the water more acidic.
ADH (antidiuretic hormone)	Hormone from pituitary gland involved in water balance in the kidneys.
aerobic respiration	Breaking down glucose in the presence of oxygen.
alleles	Different forms of a gene.
alveoli	Tiny air sacs in the lungs where gas exchange takes place. (One alveolus.)
amylase	Starch-digesting enzyme.
anaerobic respiration	Breaking down glucose without oxygen, producing lactic acid.
arteries	Blood vessel carrying blood away from the heart.
artificial selection	Producing new varieties of animals and plants by breeding selected parents. Also called selective breeding.
asexual reproduction	Reproduction involving only one parent producing genetically identical offspring or clones.
auxin	Plant hormone, important in growth and plant responses.
bacteria	Microorganisms which have a cell wall but their genetic material is not in a nucleus.
bronchioles	Small tubes branching into lungs.
capillaries	Tiny blood vessels carrying blood close to the cells and exchange substances with cells.
carbohydrase	Carbohydrate-digesting enzyme.
carbohydrate	Food type, used by the body as a source of energy.
carbon cycle	The cycling of carbon through living organisms and the environment.
carbon dioxide	Waste gas produced in respiration.
carnivores	An organism which feeds on animals.
cell	Single unit of life.
cell membrane	Controls passage of chemicals in and out of the cell.
cell wall	Wall made of cellulose surrounding and strengthening plant cells.
cellulose	Complex carbohydrate used in plant cell walls.
chlorophyll	Green pigment which absorbs energy from sunlight.
chloroplasts	Structures containing chlorophyll that capture light energy from Sun, found in some plant cells.
chromosome	Long strand of DNA found in the nucleus that carries information which controls the characteristics of an individual.
circulatory system	Network of blood vessels carrying blood around the body.
clone	Genetically identical offspring.
community	All the organisms living in a particular habitat.
consumers	Organisms which cannot make their own food and so eat other organisms.
core body temperature	Internal body temperature – about 37 °C in humans.
cornea	Transparent curved surface at the front of the eye that refracts light entering the eye.
cuttings	New plants formed from small parts of an older plant.
cytoplasm	Jelly-like material where most of the chemical reactions of the cell take place.
DDT	An insecticide which is passed along the food chain and causes damage in large mammals and birds.
decomposers	Organisms which break down the complex chemicals in dead animals and plants and recycle the nutrients.
deforestation	Cutting down forests.
detritus feeders	Organisms which feed on dead bodies and waste products.

Glossary

diabetes	Condition caused when the pancreas does not make enough insulin, or body cells do not respond properly to insulin.
diaphragm	Large sheet of muscle at bottom of thorax, important in breathing movements. Keeps the organs of the thorax and the abdomen separate.
digestive system	Group of organs carrying out digestion and absorption of the food.
DNA	The chemical which contains the coded information for life.
dominant	Character always shows even if only one allele is present.
egg	Female sex cell.
enzyme	Protein molecules which change the rate of chemical reactions in the body.
eutrophication	The death of organisms in water as a result of plant and bacterial growth due to excess nitrogen (from fertiliser or sewage) getting into the water.
excretion	Removing the waste products of the chemical reactions which go on in the body.
eye	Sense organ responding to light.
family tree	A way of showing how a characteristic is passed on through the generations.
fat	Food type, used by body for energy and as an energy store.
fertilisation	The fusing of the male and female gamete to restore the chromosome number and create a genetically new individual.
fertiliser	A mix of extra minerals, usually nitrates, put on soils to increase crop growth.
food chain	A way of linking organisms to show the feeding relationships between them.
food web	A more complex way of linking organisms in a habitat to show the feeding interrelationships.
FSH	Follicle-stimulating hormone that controls part of the menstrual cycle.
gamete	Sex cell.
gene	Small piece of DNA on a chromosome that carries the instructions for a particular characteristic.
genetic manipulation	Transferring genes from one organism to another. Also called genetic engineering.
global warming	Enhanced greenhouse effect, possibly due to build-up of carbon dioxide and other greenhouse gases in the atmosphere.
glucagon	Hormone involved in controlling blood sugar levels.
glucose	Main food used in respiration to provide energy.
greenhouse effect	Natural warming of the Earth's surface due to reflection of radiated heat back to the surface by greenhouse gases.
greenhouse gases	Gases, such as water vapour, carbon dioxide, methane, nitrous oxide, that form a layer in the Earth's atmosphere and trap heat.
growth	Making new cells.
guard cells	Cells that control the opening and closing of stomata.
gut	Digestive tract from mouth to anus.
habitat	The place where an organism lives.
haemoglobin	Red pigment in red blood cells which carries oxygen.
heart	Muscular organ that pumps blood to lungs and around the body.
herbivores	Animals that feed on plants.
heterozygous	The chromosomes in a pair have different alleles for the same gene.
homeostasis	Keeping conditions constant in the body.
homozygous	Both chromosomes in a pair have the same alleles for a gene.
hormone	Chemicals released in one part of the body and carried in the blood to have an effect somewhere else.
hypothermia	Condition when core body temperature becomes too low.
identical twins	Twins which develop after the splitting of a single fertilised egg cell.
inherited characteristics	Features passed on from one generation to the next.

Glossary

insulin	Hormone involved in controlling blood sugar levels.
kidneys	Organs which remove urea, excess water and salt from the blood to form urine.
lactic acid	Waste product of anaerobic respiration.
large intestine	Last part of gut where water is absorbed and faeces stored.
leaves	Plant organs adapted for photosynthesis.
lens	Part of the eye which can change shape and adjust focus of light on retina.
LH	Luteinising hormone that controls part of the menstrual cycle.
life processes	Seven processes which every living organism carries out: movement, response, growth, nutrition, respiration, excretion, reproduction.
lipase	Fat-digesting enzyme.
lungs	Organs of gas exchange in the chest (thorax).
meiosis	Cell division which results in a halving of the numbers of chromosomes, during formation of gametes.
menstrual cycle	Cycle of fertility in women controlled by hormones.
methane	Gas produced when vegetation rots under water and in waste gases from animals like cows and sheep.
mineral ions	Chemicals needed in minute quantities for healthy growth in animals and plants.
mitosis	Cell division which results in identical cells with identical copies of the chromosomes.
mutation	A sudden change in a gene.
natural selection	Organisms best suited to an environment are most likely to survive and reproduce, passing on their genes.
neurone	Nerve cell.
nitrates	Mineral needed for protein formation and healthy plant growth.
nitrogen cycle	The cycling of nitrogen through living organisms and the environment.
nitrogenous bases	Part of the structure of DNA: adenine, thymine, cytosine and guanine, link in pairs to join the two strands of DNA.
nucleus	Contains genetic material and controls the activities of the cell.
oestrogen	Hormone which stimulates the build-up of the lining of the womb ready for pregnancy.
optic nerve	Nerve that carries messages from the retina to the brain.
organ	Group of tissues working together to carry out a particular job.
osmosis	Movement of water along a concentration gradient through a partially permeable membrane.
ovary	Female organ that produces eggs and hormones.
oviduct	Tube connecting the ovary to the uterus.
oxygen	Gas in air needed for respiration.
oxyhaemoglobin	Haemoglobin combined with oxygen.
palisade cells	Close-packed cells near top of leaf containing many chloroplasts.
peristalsis	Muscular squeezing of gut which moves food through.
phloem	Transport tissue made of living cells which moves food around plant.
photosynthesis	Process by which plants use energy from sunlight to make food from carbon dioxide and water.
pituitary gland	Gland in brain which produces a number of hormones.
plasma	Liquid part of blood.
pollution	Things which are added to the environment which are harmful to life.
population	Group of organisms of the same species living in the same area.
predator	Animal which kills and eats other animals.
prey	Animals which are caught and eaten by predators.
primary consumer	Organism which feeds on producers
producers	Organisms which can make their own food, usually plants.

Glossary

propagator	Special enclosed space to keep cuttings damp and warm as they grow.
protease	Protein-digesting enzyme.
protein	Food type, used by the body as raw material for growth.
pulse	Pressure wave from heart contraction felt at points such as wrist and neck.
pyramid of biomass	The amount of living material at each level of a food chain, represented as a pyramid.
pyramid of energy transfer	The amount of energy in the living material at each level of a food chain.
pyramid of numbers	The number of organisms at each level in a food chain, represented as a pyramid.
receptors	Special nerve cells which respond to change in a stimulus.
recessive	Character only shows up if the allele is present in the homozygous state.
recycling	Movement of nutrients through living organisms, the air and/or the soil.
red blood cells	Cells which transport oxygen in the blood.
reflex action	Very rapid response to stimulus which does not involve conscious thought.
respiration	Releases energy from food (glucose).
retina	Layer of light-sensitive cells at the back of the eye.
root hair cell	Specialised root cell through which water and mineral ions are absorbed into a plant.
roots	Organs that anchor plants in ground, take up water and can store starch.
secondary consumer	Organism which feeds on primary or other consumers.
seed	Product of sexual reproduction in plants, it contains the new embryo plant.
sense organs	Organs that are sensitive to particular stimuli, e.g. eye.
sensitivity	Responding to changes in the surroundings.
sex chromosome	Chromosomes which determine sex, X and Y in humans.
sexual reproduction	Reproduction involving two parents and the fusing of gametes to produce genetically varying offspring.
small intestine	Main area of gut for digestion and absorption of food.
sperm	Animal male sex cell.
starch	Carbohydrate in which energy is stored in plants.
stimulus	Change in the surroundings.
stomach	Stores and mixes food with enzymes and acid.
stomata	Pores in the surface of plants through which gases move.
thermoregulatory centre	Area of brain involved in control of body temperature.
tissue culture	Producing new plants from small clumps of cells taken from an older plant
tissue	Group of similar cells together performing a particular function.
trachea	The windpipe.
transpiration	Loss of water by evaporation from the leaves of plants.
urea	Waste product of protein breakdown.
uterus	Organ which supports the developing baby during pregnancy. Also called womb.
vacuole	Permanent membrane-lined space in plant cells filled with cell sap.
vein	Blood vessel carrying blood towards the heart.
villi	Finger-like folds of the small intestine wall which increase the surface area. (One villus.)
virus	Microorganism that can only reproduce inside living cells.
xylem	Transport tissue made of dead cells which moves water around plant.